CE

# BRISTOL BRASS

# DAVID & CHARLES INDUSTRIAL HISTORY

*Brindley at Wet Earth Colliery: An Engineering Study*, by A. G. Banks and R. B. Schofield

*Bristol Brass: A History of the Industry*, by Joan Day

*The British Iron & Steel Industry: A Technical History*, by W. K. V. Gale

*The Early Factory Masters*, by Stanley D. Chapman

*The Engineering Industry of the North of Ireland*, by W. E. Coe

*A History of the Scottish Coal Industry*, Vol I 1700–1815, by Baron F. Duckham

*The History of Water Power in Ulster*, by H. D. Gribbon

*Hollins and Viyella*, by F. A. Wells

*Kenricks in Hardware*, by R. A. Church

*Uniform with*

## THE INDUSTRIAL ARCHAEOLOGY OF THE BRITISH ISLES

SERIES EDITOR: E. R. R. GREEN

*Derbyshire*, by Frank Nixon

*The East Midlands*, by David M. Smith

*Hertfordshire*, by W. Branch Johnson

*The Lake Counties*, by J. D. Marshall and M. Davies-Shiel

*Lancashire*, by Owen Ashmore

*Scotland*, by John Butt

*Southern England* (second edition, revised), by Kenneth Hudson

ASSOCIATED VOLUMES

*The Bristol Region*, by R. A. Buchanan and Neil Cossons

*Dartmoor*, by Helen Harris

*Gloucestershire Woollen Mills*, by Jennifer Tann

*Stone Blocks and Iron Rails*, by Bertram Baxter

*The Tamar Valley*, by Frank Booker

*Techniques of Industrial Archaeology*, by J. P. M. Pannell

# BRISTOL BRASS

*A History of the Industry*

JOAN DAY

DAVID & CHARLES: NEWTON ABBOT

0 7153 6065 5

TO ROY

© JOAN DAY 1973

Printed in Great Britain by
Latimer Trend & Company Ltd Plymouth
for David & Charles (Holdings) Limited
South Devon House  Newton Abbot  Devon

# Contents

# List of Illustrations

## PLATES

7

Photographs were taken by Roy Day unless otherwise acknowledged Copy photographs were made by James Robertson and Kenneth Gough

## IN TEXT

Drawings by Bo Lindner

Maps by John Doggett

Diagrams by Roy Day

# Foreword

WHEN attempts were made to establish England's first brass industry, under state monopoly in the reign of Elizabeth I, Bristol was suggested as the most suitable location for the site of the new works. Newly discovered deposits of zinc ore on Mendip were an important consideration as this was one of the raw materials needed to produce brass; abundant supplies of pit coal and the facilities of Bristol's port were additional inducements.

In the event, it proved impossible to find a vacant site in Bristol which could supply adequate water power, and the organisers turned elsewhere. Subsequently, several efforts under the state monopoly were made during the next hundred years to set up the industry in the country but with little lasting success. It was not until the eighteenth century that a permanent and prosperous brass-making industry was established under private enterprise. Again the site chosen was Bristol.

This success came shortly after improvements had been made locally in the techniques of smelting copper; thus supplies of both the raw materials necessary for brass production were available in or near the city. The new company set up at Baptist Mills was competent commercially and was soon making technical improvements in brassmaking. In consequence, Bristol gradually assumed a powerful position in the industry, which was fortified by trade agreements with companies formed in other parts of the country. Locally, production was intensified with the success of the Bristol copper works and later, with the rival company established at Warmley to exploit a newly discovered zinc-smelting process, and also to produce copper and brass.

The technical and commercial supremacy of the Bristol industry was not seriously challenged until the latter part of the eighteenth century. Large deposits of easily mined copper ore were discovered on Anglesey, which resulted in a new northern copper industry and aggravated an already difficult situation in the finances of the deep copper mines in Cornwall. This northern industry led by Thomas Williams challenged the dominance of the established trade combinations and gave encouragement to the formation of a new brass industry in Birmingham. These developments were led by able and forceful men, against whom it seems—on the little evidence available—there was no one at Bristol capable of organising any real resistance. In the difficult times which followed, the old brass company at Bristol was sold and its ownership concentrated in the hands of banking interests. From this time it was named the Harfords & Bristol Brass Company.

The resulting loss of power of the old company in the industry allowed a number of smaller businesses to come into existence at Bristol towards the end of the eighteenth century. Some of these continued the Bristol tradition for improvement in the techniques of manufacture but found that the thriving Birmingham industry, which continued to grow by adapting itself to the requirements of the Industrial Revolution in a way which they were unable to match, offered powerful opposition. By the 1840s, the last of these later Bristol businesses had succumbed to the northern competition, leaving only the diminished remains of the Harfords & Bristol Brass Company and the John Freeman & Copper Company, successor of one of the early copper businesses. The Bristol works of this last company were disposed of by 1860, and the Harfords business was sold two years later. The latter, however, continued under its old name.

From this time, there appears to have been a deliberate policy of keeping the traditional methods, which still remained in use at the old mills through lack of effective modernisation under the old management. These methods were still powered by water; slow, but cheap to run, and capable of producing high-quality goods. Many of the men who worked at the mills were descendants of original immigrants brought from the continent to start the Bristol industry. The old equipment and techniques, the traditions and the working language of the men continued at Keynsham and Saltford until the 1920s, still producing high-quality brassware. When the Avon Mill, the last brass mill of the local industry, finally closed in 1927, it was the end of over 220 years of brass manufacture.

# CHAPTER ONE

# A New Industry

'The works being brought to perfection, will cause the exportation to be as considerable to the King's revenue, as the Importation now is.'

Sir John Pettus, *Fodinae Regales* (1667)

COPPER was mined in England in prehistoric and Roman times and mining continued intermittently in the centuries that followed, but brass, the alloy of copper and zinc, was not produced in this country at all until the late sixteenth century. All earlier supplies were imported. Calamine, $ZnCO_3$, the carbonate ore of zinc which was required to blend with copper in order to produce brass, was only discovered on Mendip in June 1566 after an extensive search for it throughout the country.[1]

During the reign of Henry VIII there had been general concern at the lack of English brass and copper industries. Attempts had been made to persuade merchants, skilled in marshalling metallurgical arts, to come from Germany the acknowledged centre of European mining and metal working, to start these industries in England. Henry's plans did not materialise and the metals needed to produce cannon for national defence continued to be imported. The need to safeguard these imported materials led to a series of statutes prohibiting the re-export of copper, brass and other similar alloys.

By the reign of Elizabeth, it was clear that production of copper and brass was even more desirable, both for military and industrial requirements. The needs of the woollen trade were by now more demanding than ordnance manufacture. Large quantities of iron and brass wire were necessary to produce wool cards, the brush-like instruments with numerous wire pins set in a wooden-framed leather backing. Held in pairs, they were used for separating the tangled mass of wool so that all the fibres were interlaced but lying in the same direction; an operation carried out in preparation for spinning.

Apart from the difficulty of obtaining brass, English methods of producing wire were still extremely primitive; only manpower was available and production was very slow. The woollen industry was forced to depend on imported wire from the continent, where water-powered processes were employed which had been developed in Germany.

In 1561, approaches were made once more to German merchants on behalf of the English government. Eventually, three members of an Augsberg merchant business controlling mining in the Tyrol showed interest in extending their capital investment to England. An agreement was signed authorising a company financed by both English and German investors to search for copper and precious metals in various parts of the country. This organisation was to develop later into the Mines Royal Company. The search for copper was started and, by 1565, ores were discovered in Cumberland. Permission was obtained to bring foreign workers to start mining and smelting operations.[2]

## The Society of Mineral & Battery Works

In the same year, 1565, foundations were laid for the Society of Mineral & Battery Works. This was a very much smaller organisation but it also was to receive every encouragement from the state. The initiative came from Sir William Humfrey, Assay Master of the Mint and a shareholder in the Mines Royal Company, who introduced Christopher Schutz, manager of a calamine-mining company in Annenberg, Saxony, to run the new works. He was reported to be 'of great Cunning, Knowledge and Experience, as well in the finding of the Calamine Stone, call'd in Latin, Lapis Calaminaris, and in the right and proper use and commodity thereof, for the Composition of the mix'd metal commonly call'd Latten, and in reducing it to be soft and malleable'.[3] Humfrey petitioned for letters patent granting privileges to Schutz and himself for the whole undertaking. This included various mining projects which were not already granted to the Mines Royal Company, the exclusive mining of calamine and its use in the manufacture of brass, and the production of wire and battery from brass, iron and steel.

Battery was the name given to sheet metal, or sheet metal which had been formed into hollow-ware vessels. Both were produced in England in these early years by beating, or hammering the metal by hand. These methods were completely outdated compared with practice in Germany, as were the English wiredrawing processes. The new company petitioned for the exclusive right to use the new methods it introduced, which were to be broadly adapted from the various water-powered machines used at the time in Germany.[4]

With minor amendments, the patents were granted and sealed on 17 September 1565. At this juncture a search was started throughout the country for deposits of calamine, in which German miners assisted. Meanwhile, in Germany, Schutz sought skilled workers who were willing to travel to England to introduce the new methods, employing water-powered equipment. By June of the following year, the discovery was made which brought the brass industry to western regions. Calamine was found on Mendip in a 3ft wide vein on Worle Hill, on land belonging to Sir Henry Wallop. When tested, the ore was found to be superior in quality and yield to most supplies in use on the continent and, subsequently, further deposits were discovered in the area.

The Mendip discovery changed the future of the company, whose members had been on the point of despair at finding English calamine, and were about to set up their works at Wandsworth. From there, they could have imported supplies through the port of London, from Aachen, otherwise known as Aix-la-Chapelle, a traditional source on the continent.[5]

Now, a suitable site was sought within easy reach of the Mendip

B

plateau. Nearby, at Bristol, fuel supplies were good and cheap, and pit coal was mined within four miles of the city. Moreover, water-borne transport was available from the Forest of Dean where good-quality iron could be obtained. As the company planned to manufacture wire from iron in addition to brass, these advantages were of great importance. The Earl of Pembroke, one of the principal shareholders representing the government, was in favour of using the mill site available at Bristol Castle. He made every effort to encourage this plan but later investigations proved the water power to be inadequate to run the new machinery.[6]

Following the rejection of Bristol Castle as a suitable site for the works, the company 'were forced to search the country by Severn side more than 40 miles. And finding all the pleasant rivers set full of grist and tucking mills . . . crossed the Severn to view the rivers of Usk and Wye in Wales . . .'[7] A site was discovered eventually, lying partly on the Earl of Pembroke's land on the Angiddy Brook at Tintern. Towards the end of 1566, the building of the wire-making house, two forges and an annealing furnace was said to be well forward and expected to be complete by the end of the year. Christopher Schutz felt justified in promising the production of 25cwt of iron wire per week, and 40cwt of brass wire; enough, he estimated, to repay quickly the building charges of the works.[8]

More than a year passed, however, before brassmaking was reported at Tintern. The occasion was marked by the presence of several shareholders of the company, and the Governor of the Company of Mines Royal. On the first attempt, it was stated that the works had succeeded in producing a brass which added 28lb to every hundredweight of copper used. This was the usual method of assessing the success of the early brassmakers' art, as it was thought to be of prime importance to make best use of the copper, which was by far the most costly constituent. Two days later, in trials, the increase on copper was reported to be in the order of 35lb in the hundredweight.

These results appear to indicate complete success in the first attempts at making English brass, but not all was as well as the report suggested. The processes concerning brass at the Tintern works were never developed further, and the brass works there were never completed. Some thirty years later, it was explained that the brass furnaces produced a metal of the right colour, but it could not be made malleable.[9] Without this property it would have been impossible to produce brass sheet by the battery method. This, in turn, would have prevented the manufacture of wire, as it was necessary to cut sheets of brass into narrow strips which were then rounded and drawn through a series of holes made progressively smaller.

The proportions of copper to zinc in the metal reported at the first Tintern trials should have resulted in a malleable brass, unless impurities were present which had a harmful effect.[10] The men blamed the failure on the quality of the English calamine stone, but this was used later with great success. A possible cause may be indicated by the interest of Christopher Schutz in using pit coal as his fuel.[11] The use of coal for this purpose was not fully understood at this time and, if used incorrectly, the resulting sulphurous fumes could have affected the malleability of brass produced at Tintern. Alternatively, the impurities may have been introduced in the copper provided by the Mines Royal Company.

As the future plans for making brass at Tintern were abandoned, the remains of the 20 to 30 tons of calamine brought from Mendip were stored for a number of years, then used eventually for mending gaps in the fishing weir in the river.[12] Further development at the works revolved around the manufacture of iron wire, which posed extra difficulties as Schutz was inexperienced in this kind of production.

In May 1568, the two companies formed with the purpose of establishing new metalliferous industries received their charters of incorporation. Both had been organised on the joint-stock principle, with the capital of the partners pooled for the benefit of the business. They were the first joint-stock enterprises in the country to be concerned with home manufacture, as distinct from the established trading companies with specified rights in lands overseas. The creation of these privileged companies provided the security for the introduction of foreign capital, and enabled the formation of special monopolies. Thus, the previous grants and exclusive rights were endorsed, and strengthened in some cases, giving the Mineral & Battery Works very far-reaching privileges. These still included the sole right to mine calaminc and make brass, and to produce wire and battery by means of the new water-powered machines which the company had  introduced.[13]

The granting of the charter made no significant change in activities at Tintern but, at the end of 1569, Humfrey and Schutz gave up their claims, and a lease was granted to others more capable of taking over the iron-wire works. Brass manufacture was completely ignored until 1582, when Sir Richard Martyn, a London alderman and shareholder of the company, offered the Mineral & Battery Works the sum of £50 per annum for a lease of the right to mine calamine and to make brass battery. The offer was taken up at the time, but developments were held in abeyance until 1587, when the agreement was ratified. It concerned a group of four partners led by Martyn, and including John Brode a London goldsmith, who had been experimenting with brassmaking for a number of years, using imported rough copper. Now, battery works were erected at Queen's Mill at Isleworth, consisting of 'divers working houses, melting hearths, waterworks, furnaces and other engines with great bellows, stampers and other preparations meet and necessary to be used for the handling of the works of the making, melting and casting of metals'.[14]

Very soon there was disagreement between the partners, who declared that Brode took possession of stock and also concealed profit, moreover, the Society of Mineral & Battery Works were alienated by his continued refusal to reveal his secrets of making brass. Despite these difficulties the business flourished for a number of years, using new sources of calamine discovered in the

Mendip area, particularly at Brockley and Broadfield Down near Wrington. It was later claimed that the weekly production at Isleworth consumed 18cwt copper and 36cwt calamine, yielding 25cwt brass, and 2cwt spillings or waste, per week. The costs were £62 6s; the brass sold for £3 per cwt, the spillings for 50s per cwt, giving a total gross income of £80 per week. The cost of producing 10cwt of battery, using five men, was 25s, and the resulting plates of brass were then worth an additional 24s per cwt. It was said that a clear profit of £26 19s had been gained weekly from the works.[15]

Having thus created a successful business, Brode tried to force his remaining partners to sell out to him, and from April 1596, decided to pay no further fees to the Society of Mineral & Battery Works. The company declared his lease void and, subsequently, granted it to others; but Brode then retaliated by refusing to release his stocks of calamine for use by the new lessees. The dispute was long and acrimonious. In 1605, at the end of his resources after continued legal action, Brode finally stated to the House of Lords that by the grace of God he was 'the first man here in England that comixed copper and calamine, and brought it to perfection to abide the hammer and be beaten into plates and raised into kettles and pans by hammers driven by water. The company have taken the works out of the hands of Englishmen and put it into the hands of strangers ... and thereby the price of that metal is double [what] it was in Queen Elizabeth's time'.[16]

The strangers to whom Brode referred were Abraham van Herrick, a Dutch merchant, together with his partners, who were granted a lease and had constructed works at Rotherhithe. This system of leasing was to become the established pattern of development for the brass industry of the country throughout most of the seventeenth century for, in 1604, despite severe criticism in Parliament of the exclusive privilege of monopolies, the Society of Mineral & Battery Works was able to renew its charter. Thus, still in possession of the sole right of calamine mining and brass manufacture, the company continued to lease the privilege to those interested in paying for it. The businesses organised in this way failed to supply the needs of the country, and few flourished for many years. Although various import restrictions were put into force, foreign brass and brassware continued to be imported.[17]

### Unlawful Business

Throughout the period of inadequate home supplies during the seventeenth century several cases of illegal manufacture of brass and brassware were discovered, including works which were operating without leases near Bristol.

In July 1629, officials learned from another lessee that there were 'certain works contrarie to their privileges set up in or about Bristol called the brass works, wherein they make wire and other things . . . with Water wheels and such other Engines and Tools as are used by the Company, and that one of their workmen at Tintern is gon thither to them'.[18] Two members of the company were instructed to visit the illicit sites during a forthcoming journey to Tintern. Letters were sent to William Berry and John Bisse, advising them that their works at Stapleton and Cheddar must be demolished. The command had not been carried out by the end of the year, neither had the two men appeared as directed before the company to answer the charges. Following a petition to the Privy Council, a messenger was sent to collect Berry and Bisse from Bristol and, later, both made due submission and acknowledgement of their offences. They also made offers of annual rent for the privilege of manufacture and, shortly afterwards, a lease was granted to William Berry to make brass wire, on annual payment of 70 nobles.[19]

No further references in the court books were made to William Berry or the watermill and works at Stapleton, and it can be inferred that his business probably continued for at least the ten-year term of the lease. The granting of a similar lease to John Bisse was delayed without any explanation, but a few weeks later he was allowed the privilege of manufacturing brass wire. For the

first year only, his rent was reduced to a peppercorn but this provision was made on condition that he refrained from making iron
wire contrary to the company's privilege, or enticing away any of
the company's workmen. His request to mine calamine was held
over.[20]

By February of the following year, it was discovered that John
Bisse had secretly purchased a large store of nail rods in the
Forest of Dean, from Sir John Wintour who was also suspected of
working illegally. When Bisse was accused of abusing the privilege
of the society by making iron wire from the rods, he made a request
for a lease to manufacture such wire, explaining that his production
was not planned for public sale, but to lessees of the company. As
foreign wire was now prohibited, he suggested that existing works
could not supply the needs of the country. He was supported by
a petition from the cardmakers and wiredrawers of Bristol, who
complained that they had been kept short of wire by the manufacturers of the company. Indeed, only the previous year, the society
had dealt with a report of 500qr of foreign wire being seized in
Bristol.[21]

The governors of the society were no longer willing to listen to
Bisse, and declared his petition to be a fraud. In July 1631, it was
ordered that his works at Cheddar should be demolished. Later in
the year, when proof was presented that the orders had been carried
out and Bisse had promised not to manufacture any further supplies of wire, they allowed 'some charitable consideration' to his
family as reparation.[22]

Similar discoveries of illegal works were made in other parts of
the country but one, at Esher in Surrey, is relevant to later developments in Bristol. There, from about 1649, Jacob Mummer
from Germany was working a brass plate and wire mill. He found
it necessary to import his copper from Sweden, as the refining
activities of the Mines Royal Company at Keswick had long been
in decline, and were completely halted by the Civil War.[23] In
1656, he appealed to Parliament for a reduction of duties on copper

imported from Sweden and, six years later, was again concerned in
a joint petition to Parliament, with Daniel Demetrius and Peter
Hoote, for assistance for the brass industry. They stated that the
manufacture of brass was almost lost throughout the country, and
that 'their fires were going out'. This gave rise to another petition
presented three years later requesting further protection against
imported brassware, but no action was taken by the government
on any of these requests.[24]

Despite the decline in the English brass industry caused by the
difficulty in obtaining copper, the search for calamine continued,
with large amounts being exported to brass producers on the continent. In 1662, John Tripp was summoned to appear before the
court of the society to explain why he had been 'meddling with
and transporting Calamine Stone beyond the Seas' when he had no
licence. He pleaded ignorance of the company's authority, and explained that his supplies were obtained 12 miles from Bristol on
Mendip where it was very plentiful. He obtained 400 to 500 tons
annually, and offered to deliver calamine, already calcined, to the
company at £3 10s per ton, or pay a percentage royalty on each ton
sold elsewhere. The company took up his second offer and agreed
that he should pay 5s for each ton sold or transported, provided
that all transactions were recorded in the Customs House in Bristol.
Later, after discussion on the quality of English calamine compared
with the continental product, the court invited John Tripp to send
a barrel of his calcined ore to London for tests at the first opportunity.[25]

During these exchanges there were no references to the locality
of Tripp's mines on Mendip, but contemporary sources make it
quite clear that calamine was being mined at Wrington, Row-
berrow, Shipham, Winscombe and Burrington parishes.[26] Another
lease was contracted by the society in June 1664, for mining calamine north of Bristol. It was granted to a Mr Locke for twenty-one
years, allowing him to work ore in the parish of Almondsbury in
Gloucestershire.[27]

### The Mines Royal Act

Sir John Pettus, one of the members of the Society of Mineral & Battery Works showed particular concern at the worsening state of the English brass industry, and tried to raise some official support in his *Fodinae Regales* of 1667. Again in 1683, writing of English calamine, he remarked, 'we have mountains of it [of better quality than in any part of Europe, yet] we let the Calaminaris go for Ballast into foreign parts in very great Quantities, before it be wrought, so as the best Brass beyond the Seas is made of our stone rather than their own'.[28]

In face of this rapid deterioration in the production of both copper and brass, legislation was finally passed in 1689 limiting the powers of the privileged companies. This Mines Royal Act had the effect of encouraging immediate activity in the mining and working of copper, by stating that no mine of copper, tin, lead or iron was in future to be considered the monopoly of the Crown. An additional Act was passed in 1693 to prevent any possible dispute, so clearing the way for private initiative.[29]

# CHAPTER TWO

# *Bristol Initiative*

'In 1702, the . . . Brass works . . . was erected near Bristol, which has continued to this time, but with great additions and improvements; and this is now perhaps the most considerable brass house in all Europe.'

Thomas Williams, Member of the House, in evidence to a House of Commons Committee (April 1799)

AT the close of the seventeenth century, Bristol was a thriving commercial centre, with a large port second only to London. Supplies from widely surrounding areas were sent to Bristol to be manufactured into goods and distributed overseas and inland. Here too was the focus for the production and marketing of lead, a trade encouraged by the close proximity of the Mendip lead-mines.

## The Copper Smelters

### THE CLERKES' ACTIVITIES

In the 1670s, important discoveries were patented which improved the reverberatory furnace, enabling pit coal to be employed in the lead-smelting works at Bristol. Sir Clement Clerke was one of those concerned in the development; but because of difficulties encountered with patent rights, he turned to the smelting of other metals, assisted by his son Talbot. They concentrated more particularly on the production of copper in the coal-fired reverberatory furnace, and a new process was patented by them in 1687. The nature of the improvement made is, unfortunately, not recorded, but it has been suggested that it concerned the construction of the

26

furnace chimney, or perhaps the type of coal fuel employed. John Coster and Gabriel Wayne are believed to have assisted in the practical work of the new development.[1]

By 1688, the Clerkes had a supply of copper available for sale at London, thought to have been an experimental production from Stockley Vale, Bristol, the family works formerly used for their lead-smelting operations. Thus, in this pioneer method, one of the main difficulties of smelting copper brought about by the rising costs of wood fuel, had apparently been eliminated by an improvement in the use of pit coal.

The Mines Royal Act which, as we have seen, was to encourage development in the mining and working of metals, passed through Parliament the following year. Two years later, new works were established upstream of Tintern, on the River Wye at Upper Redbrook, near small deposits of copper ore which had been discovered in the Forest of Dean.[2] John Coster's father had been connected with ironworks in this area and now the son, one of Sir Clement's former assistants, returned to take responsibility for a new organisation, the joint-stock company of the Copper Works of Upper Redbrook. The site, previously a paper mill, was leased by Henry Benedict Hall to Coster and his associates who consisted of ten London merchants, headed by William Dockwray.[3]

William Dockwray, or Dockwra, established another partnership the following year with works at Esher on the River Mole in Surrey. It seems very likely that he took the premises formerly set up by Jacob Mummer, but it has not been possible to trace the connection. Certainly, the production of brass at Esher was continued, and was now described as being

compos'd with about two sevenths of fine copper, four sevenths of lapis calaminaris, and one seventh of shruff, which is old plate brass. This put into pots containing ten or twelve pounds of metal each, and set in a furnace, where there is freedom of air at bottom, melts and coalizes, or joins in ten or twelve hours time into a new thing called brass. Then eight or ten of these small pots are poured into one larger; and when 'tis perfectly digested, and well scumm'd from the dross, 'tis then poured between two stones of a tun weight, or more

each, which are elevated at one end for to make the metal fill the whole vacuity,
and then 'tis set horizontal to cool, and thence comes out a plate of about
seventy pounds weight.[4]

The works manufactured its sheet metal in a rolling mill, an
innovation for the industry, and in subsequent processes made
brass wire using twenty-four drawing benches in its wiremills. Wire
was employed to manufacture pins, a product in which the company specialised, making this establishment the first comprehensive
works of its kind.

These flourishing mills at Esher were undoubtedly of great
importance in the country's industry of the 1690s, but after the
turn of the century, little was heard of them. Dockwray had been
Comptroller of the Penny Post in 1697, but following inquiries,
was dismissed in 1700 for providing an unsatisfactory service.[5] He
later showed signs of financial embarrassment, but while in the
brass and copper business, was said to have been responsible for
the production of 80 tons of copper per annum, equal to the output
of all other English smelting concerns. It has been assumed that this
copper was produced at his Esher works, but it seems more likely
that he obtained his supplies from the works at Upper Redbrook.
Under the management of John Coster this business continued to
thrive, but subsequently, in deeds where its partners are listed, it is
noticeable that Dockwray's name is missing.[6]

Meanwhile, during this decade, the effect of the Mines Royal Act
was encouraging several other companies in the mining and smelting of copper. Of those which are relevant to Bristol, the English
Copper Company set up its works at Lower Redbrook, quite close
to John Coster's site. This company later stated to a House of
Commons inquiry, that it purchased the right to use the furnaces
patented by the Clerkes. At its Lower Redbrook works, the company was assisted technically for a period by Gabriel Wayne, formerly with John Coster in the service of Sir Clement Clerke.[7]

Later activities of the Clerkes in the copper-smelting industry
are a little obscure. Sir Clement Clerke died in 1693 with his

financial affairs in an involved state, but in the previous year, his son Talbot had been connected with the formation of a 'new Company for Smelting downe Lead with Pitt coale'. It took over the Clerke's smelting premises situated at Stockley Vale down-stream of Bristol, but this failed owing to bad management although the concern went on to develop a highly successful business as the London Lead Company.[8] In 1695, the site was returned to Sir Talbot but it was later reported that he did not re-sume lead smelting. In 1698, there are brief references to a Thomas Clarke concerned in the smelting of copper at Bristol, which can be assumed to refer to the business of Sir Talbot Clerke, and during this period he was also involved in a partnership for copper smelting in Cornwall which proved unsuccessful and was soon abandoned.[9] It was Gabriel Wayne, one of the Clerke's former assistants who, at Conham, was to be responsible for introducing a thriving copper industry to the Bristol area.

ACTIVITIES AT CONHAM

In May 1696, the *Mary* of St Ives set sail from Truro with a cargo of 34 tons of mundic ore for Abraham Elton at Bristol. Other supplies simply described as copper ore were to follow shortly, suggesting that a new copper works had been established in the city. Two years later, Thomas Cletscher, a Swedish mining official, visited the site, which he described as lying 2 miles east of Bristol. This later proved to be Conham, upstream of the city on the banks of the Avon, where the river was still navigable. Abraham Elton, a successful merchant, was in partnership there with Gabriel Wayne, Clerke's former assistant and technical adviser at Lower Redbrook.[10]

Cletscher had his difficulties in being allowed to see the works but, overcoming these, he recorded details of the furnace con-struction and methods used for smelting. He found three melting-houses at Conham, each containing three reverberatory furnaces built of brick and bound with iron straps to withstand the severe heat. They stood 4ft high above the foundations; each interior was lined with firebrick made of clay from Windsor, with the main ore chamber measuring 3ft square and 2ft in height. In the vaulted roof was an opening for charging the ore, and a door along the side of the furnace enabled the loading of coal; the taphole was on the opposite side. Other smaller apertures were placed for stirring ores, and for inspection. The firebox at one end of the ore chamber, 3ft by $1\frac{1}{2}$ft, had a grating of iron bars which allowed ash to fall into the deep pit underneath. Through an opening on one side of this pit, the fire drew its air supply which took the flames over the crosswall separating the firebox from the main chamber, to follow the curved line of the vaulted roof to the opposite end, where a chimney provided the necessary draught.

The ores were first of all calcined, or heated to a point short of melting; a process carried on outside the melting houses, in separate furnaces for a period of up to eight days. The ore was then friable and easily stamped or crushed to a fine state, ready for melting. It was then transferred in 4 to 5cwt loads to a pre-heated melting furnace, with a quantity of lime added as a flux. All apertures were stopped up, and a fierce heat applied for about three hours until the ore began to melt. It was then stirred and the furnace was resealed. When the ore was fully melted, the heat was reduced and the resulting mass was left until the metal had sunk to the bottom. The slag floating on the surface was removed, then the metal was tapped.

The mass resulting from this first operation, called the matte, was stamped, but not calcined further, before loading into another melting furnace already prepared for the purpose. After another four hours it was tapped again, and at this stage usually produced a black copper. If the ore was particularly suitable it could yield a metal similar to refined copper at this stage, but more usually it was refined in a smaller reverberatory furnace, taking 15 to 20cwt. The refining furnaces were similar to those used for melting and the process much the same except for the more moderate heat used.

The resulting copper produced by these means was usually up to 92 per cent pure.

In addition to ore from Cornwall, the works was probably receiving copper from the rich mines of North Molton, in North Devon. In 1698, they had been working for about four years, producing 4,000 to 5,000 tons of ore per annum, which sold at £6 to £8 10s per ton. It was taken by packhorse to Barnstaple at a cost of 2s per ton, and from there by small boat to Bideford, at 6d per ton. It was then shipped direct to London, at 10s per ton, or to Bristol at 2s 6d to 3s per ton. Bristol purchasers were said to provide the most reliable market for the ore which, Cletscher wrote, normally contained up to 30 per cent copper, sometimes 40 per cent or more. He regarded the mines of Truro as very inferior to those of North Molton, producing only 10 per cent copper, which he found was 'considered as little in England', but this was also sold mainly to Bristol at £4 per ton.[11]

Cletscher was critical of the metal produced by the Bristol methods, describing it as fragile or brittle, and blackish compared with the Swedish product. He attributed this to the sulphurous fumes absorbed from coal, and noted that the local coppersmiths complained that it was difficult to work. He mentioned particularly that it was not suitable for making brass, but might be improved if charcoal was used to fuel the refining stages. But these were early days at Conham, and there were many improvement yet to come.

Although critical of the technical ability he found, Cletscher considered Bristol to be the most convenient place in the country for such a works, because coal mined locally could be bought for half the price it fetched elsewhere, a mere 10s per chaldron. Each furnace could be manned by one master at 12s per week and a man at 8s per week. He noted that it was also easy to market the products locally and to export through the port of Bristol.

The newly successful manufacturers were, however, finding difficulty in marketing their total output. Nevertheless, they were encouraged to increase production by their quickly developing expertise. At the time of Cletscher's visit in 1698, Abraham Elton was seeking a contract from the Lords of the Treasury to produce new coinage for the country. In this he was unsuccessful, and he must have continued to search diligently for further outlets for his stocks of copper.[12] A large proportion of copper produced in other countries at this period was taken up in producing brass, but this market was not available to the English copper smelters. William Dockwray's works had its own supplies and at the time was the country's only brass works of consequence. The main stocks of brass metal and wares were still imported from the Low Countries, a situation which was to alter during the early decades of the eighteenth century when developments initiated at Bristol proved to be the start of a new era in the British manufacture of brass.

## The Brass Manufacturers

### ABRAHAM DARBY AND BAPTIST MILLS

Bristol was developing into a stronghold of the Quaker faith of the Religious Society of Friends and, undoubtedly, this was a factor which influenced Abraham Darby to set up business in the area. He came from a Quaker family of farmers and nailmakers near Dudley in the Midlands and moved to Bristol in 1699, after completing his Birmingham apprenticeship as a maker of malt-mills.[13] The maltmill business which Darby established in Bristol at the turn of the century appears to have been a new trade in the city, thus he experienced little opposition in starting the new works. The mill he produced was probably similar to a coffee-mill, with a central cutting screw in some kind of container for preparing the domestic supply of ale. Houghton had noted in the early 1690s that this useful piece of household equipment was available from Birmingham, where Darby had carried out his apprenticeship.[14]

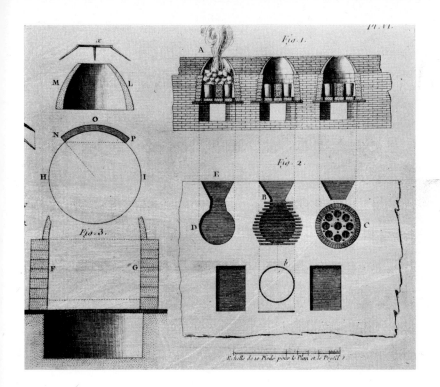

Page 33 *Illustrations from* L'Art de Convetir le Cuivre Rouge ou le Cuivre Rosette en Laiton ou Cuivre Jaune, *by J. Galon (1764), showing equipment similar to that used at Bristol:* (above) *the calamine-brass furnaces;* (below) *the battery mill*

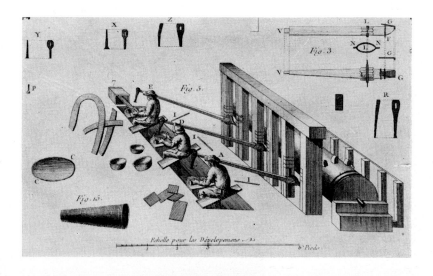

Page 34 (left) *A sketch of Crew's Hole copper works by Reinhold Angerstein, 1754;* (below) *the Troopers Hill chimney above Crew's Hole*

Within the first year of his Bristol business, Darby himself took an apprentice, John Thomas, a Quaker from Dolobran in North Wales. His former master, Charles Lloyd, had given him a recommendation to go to Edward Lloyd of Bristol, to look for new employment. Shortly after arriving in Bristol, Thomas started to work for Darby and later became his valued assistant.[15] Through this connection, the Quaker cidermaker Edward Lloyd may have been given his opportunity to meet Abraham Darby. At this period, Edward Lloyd was one of five partners, all Bristol Quakers, who were interested in starting a brass works. On 25 July 1700, they petitioned the Privy Council, declaring their wish to manufacture brass, and praying for a Charter of Incorporation.[16] Nothing emerged from this petition, and those concerned with Lloyd withdrew their interest, but later developments in the Bristol industry involved both Lloyd and Darby.

The early years of Darby's Bristol business are not well documented, and dates that are recorded prove rather conflicting, but it can be inferred that by 1702–3 he was concerned with brass production.[17] It may have been that he wished to make some component for his maltmill manufacture, possibly the container, and been persuaded to experiment; or perhaps his interest was roused by Edward Lloyd, but there is no evidence on these points. Whatever his purpose in producing brass, he was in an ideal situation for such an enterprise. Apart from the commercial advantages of Bristol, the local smelters were seeking new markets in which to dispose of their stocks of copper; they may even have offered him encouragement. Calamine, the other raw material required for making brass was readily available just twelve to fifteen miles away.

At the time of these early attempts in the manufacture of brass, Darby set out to acquire the skills of workers from an area where such trades were traditional. In an account written in her later years, Hannah Rose, daughter of apprentice John Thomas, described how Darby 'went over to Holland and hired some Dutch workmen, and set up the Brass works at Baptist Mills'.[18] This site

C

was north-east of the boundaries of Bristol on the River Frome, a tributary of the Avon which it joined a mile or so downstream in the centre of the city. These men from Holland (and perhaps other parts of the Low Countries which all tended to be described as Dutch), would have provided all the skills needed to make calamine brass, as manufactured in their own countries. They would also have been practised at casting large flat plates of brass by pouring molten metal into moulds formed by large slabs of granite, but their experience of foundry work probably ended there.[19] At this early date, the casting of ornaments, bells and cannon in bronze and other copper alloys was a specialised craft, not used in a brass works, and the art of casting domestic wares in brass was not exploited until very much later. In Darby's day, the manufacture of utensils from brass involved beating the comparatively soft metal into shape.[20]

The next stage in the work at Baptist Mills after the casting of plates would have been the formation of thin sheets of brass. Rolling had been used for this purpose some eight years before at the Esher brass and copper works, but there is no mention of this new technique in the early years at Bristol. It seems more likely that the Dutch workers would have beaten the plates of brass into thin sheets by means of water-powered battery hammers.[21] These sheets were then used to manufacture battery, the principal product of the Bristol works and which, by this date, usually meant beaten hollow-ware vessels. The single sheets of brass were still 'battered' by hand-held hammer in many parts of England, but the Dutch were skilled operators of fast water-powered hammers.[22] This was one of the factors which enabled the Low Countries to be the largest exporters of brass hollow-ware, which was in constant demand for both domestic and industrial purposes, and particularly for re-export to the English plantations. This lead of the Dutch was now about to be challenged by the works developing in the Bristol area.

Some Dutch workers were soon installed at an additional mill on the River Avon at Keynsham, 5 miles south-east of the centre of Bristol. There, in January 1708, John Buck, described as a brassworker and the first so mentioned, registered the birth of his son at St John's Church.[23] A month later, a birth in the Steger family was recorded. This was one of the Dutch families which were to become well known in connection with the brass mills throughout their history. With skilled men working at this new site, the ample waters of the Avon could be utilised to drive battery hammers, providing a more reliable source of power than could be supplied at Baptist Mills by the fluctuating River Frome.[24]

In the early stages of development, three Quaker partners were jointly concerned in the enterprise with Abraham Darby. As well as Edward Lloyd, the cidermaker who had taken responsibility for John Thomas joining the works, there were John Andrews, a vintner whose sister Elizabeth was married to Lloyd, and Arthur Thomas, a Bristol pewterer, originally from Barrow, south of Bristol. Hannah Rose described Darby as the 'active man' of the partnership.[25] These four men 'had for severall years then past jointly carried on the Trade or Art of Making Brass or Battery and other Matters relating to a Brass work',[26] when a deed of partnership was drawn up establishing a company of eight proprietors on 30 November 1706.

The four existing partners were now joined by Benjamin Coole, a Bristol merchant who came from Devizes; Richard Stafford, Bristol merchant, formerly a mercer from Lougharne, South Wales, married to Mary, sister of John Andrews; John Hitchcock, Bristol needlemaker; Abraham Lloyd, mariner, possibly related to Edward Lloyd. All were of the Quaker persuasion.[27]

It was agreed that the mills and other unspecified property of the former company should be transferred to the new proprietors, and existing stock valued at £5,836 2s 6½d should be increased to a value of £8,000, with provision for a further increase up to a limit of £12,000. This new organisation was to be a joint-stock company with transferable shares, and a transfer book was to be

kept where sales of shares were to be carefully recorded. Arrangements were made for the time when the number of proprietors
would exceed fourteen, when a committee of five was to be elected
in order to run the company. Thus the re-organisation of the brass
works in Bristol, still as yet unnamed, was under way.[28]

This new company may have been initiated by the fact that
Darby's interest was already moving away from brass battery
towards hollow-ware vessels of a different kind. Cast in iron, such
wares could be very much cheaper to produce and for most purposes just as suitable. Hannah Rose described Darby's investigations:

> After some time he had a mind to set the Dutchmen to try to cast Iron Pots in
> sand. They tried several times but could not do it, so he was at a great loss in
> paying Wages for no result. At length, John Thomas, my Father, then a young
> Man who came on trial to learn the trade of Malt Mill making, seeing the
> Dutchmen try and could not bring to perfection, asked his Master to let him
> try, so with his leave he did it, and afterwards his Master and him were bound
> in Articles in the year 1707, that John Thomas should be bound to work at
> that business and keep it secret and not teach anybody else, for three years.
> They were so private as to stop the keyhole of the Door.[29]

The remaining brass-works proprietors did not share Darby's
enthusiasm for cast-iron ware and were not to be drawn into this
new manufacture. When he found that they were quite unwilling
to extend the business and include his new methods, Darby decided
to withdraw from the works; probably doing so about 1708 when
Quaker records of his children's births indicate that he moved
from outside the boundaries into the city itself.[30] He worked for
some time in an iron foundry set up in Cheese Lane in the city,
and was without the support of partners until James Peters and
Griffin Prankhard joined him in 1710.[31]

By the time of the new partnership agreement, Darby had
already extended his business by taking over an established blast
furnace in Coalbrookdale in Shropshire, and was in the process of
gradually removing men and materials there. Coalbrookdale was a
more suitable area for the work he was about to undertake. There,

from 1709, Darby was making use of coke as fuel for his blast furnace, carbonising low-sulphur coal locally available, and thus freeing himself from the difficulty of obtaining sufficient supplies of charcoal. In achieving success in this new technique, where others before him had tried and failed, he was responsible for one of the most important developments in the industrial use of pit coal as a fuel.[32]

This success of Darby's use of coke has led to speculation on the contribution he may have made to the technique of brass-making before he left Baptist Mills. He probably had knowledge of the use of coke from his apprentice days as a maltmill maker, for the malt trade was one of the first industries to use coked pit coal as a fuel. When he came to Bristol, he settled in an area where the use of coal fuels in reverberatory furnaces had been successfully pioneered for the smelting of both lead and copper, and where these techniques were still evolving towards the use of coke as a fuel. Dr R. A. Mott has suggested that Darby must have been responsible for the use of coal in place of charcoal in the brassmaking process at Baptist Mills. Possibly he introduced the coking of the coal fuel inside the brass furnace as a preliminary process of making brass, a procedure which, once established, remained in practice until the end of the era of calamine brass.[33]

Darby's successful introduction of coke to his Coalbrookdale furnace almost immediately after leaving Bristol suggests that he learned the value of low-sulphur coal while still in the city. most certainly, large quantities of coal were being consumed in his Bristol brass furnaces. Arthur Thomas gave evidence to a parliamentary committee that over 400 horseloads of coal were used per week by the Bristol brass works between 1710 and 1712.[34] This was in addition to the fuel requirements of the local copper works.

By the time of Thomas's report, Abraham Darby had withdrawn his interests from the Cheese Lane foundry and was concentrating on Coalbrookdale but had not entirely lost his interest in the production of non-ferrous metals. In April 1710 he made an agreement in Shropshire for mining rights of copper and other minerals at Harmear Hill, on the property of the Countess of Bridgwater.[35] Some of Darby's associates were among eight partners who founded the Tern Works in Shropshire in 1710. The venture was mainly concerned with working iron, but also produced brass and rolled brass plate, and was described as the first joint works of its kind in the country.[36] It does not, however, appear to have ever been a challenge to the Bristol brass works and, later, little was heard of it.

BRISTOL AND ESHER AMALGAMATION

When Darby withdrew as 'active man' from Baptist Mills about 1708, it could be suspected that he left a void that was difficult to fill. Nevertheless, the brass company continued to thrive and to make technical progress, although it is not known who assumed the responsibility.

Towards the close of the following year, on 30 September 1709, the Company for Brass & Battery Work at Bristol (named in a document for the first time), 'entered into a union and coalition with John Coggs and others, his co-partners, in a Brass Wire work at Esher in Surrey'.[37] These works may have been the large copper and brasswire works which belonged to William Dockwray in the 1690s, but it has not been possible to verify this. The share-out of stock of the two businesses after the amalgamation indicates that the Esher works was small in comparison, or perhaps rather run down. The agreement allowed for the 64 shares of the Bristol company to be brought up to 80 at the new liaison, with 12 to be reserved for John Coggs and his business partners.

The total value of the two businesses amounted to £15,953 1s 10d, and provision was made to increase this in the future to a sum not exceeding £50,000. The proprietors in the company thereafter were deemed to hold shares in the 'General Joint United Stock of the Societies of Bristol and Esher for Making Brass, Battery and Brass wire'.[38]

The name of Esher was retained for a long period in the title of the company,[39] but little was heard of the wire works there in connection with the Bristol business. Wire production eventually became the largest part of the production at Bristol, manufactured at Avon Mill, Keynsham, but it did not assume any importance for many years to come. For the time, the emphasis at Bristol remained firmly on the production of battery.

PETITION FOR PROTECTION

Although the manufacture of batteryware at Bristol had become well established by the first decade of the eighteenth century, the proprietors were soon complaining against the system of duties on imported wares. The works still had difficulties in producing the quality of brass required, and while large quantities were being made at Bristol, foreign brass continued to come into the country because of its superior working properties. In 1712, a group of copper and brass manufacturers combined together to petition Parliament in an effort to obtain protection from this competition.

Bristol played a prominent part in the petition, which was presented to the House under the names of Abraham Elton, co-partner of the Bristol copper business; Benjamin Coole, Edward Lloyd and John Hitchcock, all proprietors of the brass works in Bristol; John Shorey of the Temple Mills brass and copper works near Marlow; and John Knight, whose affiliations are unknown.[40]

The manufacturers claimed that they provided employment for many thousands of the country's poor. Where formerly all goods they produced were imported from Holland, now they were made by English people, and from English copper and calamine. Because of encouragement granted by old laws to foreign goods at a time when none was produced in this country, they now faced disadvantages, particularly when exporting wares to the plantations. Under the existing 'drawback' system, duties on brassware imported from Holland were almost entirely repaid to merchants if the goods were re-exported. In consequence, Dutch battery bought in this country for £7 10s per cwt, having paid duty of £1 10s 4d, could obtain £1 6s in drawback on being re-exported for the colonial market, making it cheaper than English brassware priced at £7 per cwt.[41]

Another complaint was against Dutch black battery, which escaped paying fair custom duty by being described as 'metal-prepared'. The petitioners claimed that this particular term was an ancient one intended to denote ingots or lumps of brass metal, whereas the Dutch imports under this category contained dull, but otherwise finished, batteryware. It only lacked the last brightening process, estimated to cost about 1s per cwt, but by using the 'metal-prepared' description, saved 11s per cwt duty. A similar situation occurred with dull brass sheet, and unfinished 'bottoms' of vessels, both classified as 'black lattin'. The petitioners pressed for these goods to bear the same duty as finished battery.[42]

Merchants importing these goods from the continent, and craftsmen making use of brass metal, banded together to counter-petition, declaring that if extra duties were imposed, the country would suffer from inferior wares which could result from English brass. An essay published at the time discussed the arguments of both sides, and also referred to an attack on the religion of the industry's Quaker leaders and the strength of that faith in the Bristol area.[43] Forceful arguments were presented for retaining the duties at existing levels in support of the country's woollen trade: if Dutch brass was allowed to continue entering the country in exchange for the right to export cloth to Holland, the English economy would be less likely to suffer.

The House of Commons appointed a committee to enquire into the different aspects of evidence provided by the opposing parties, and a large amount of information on the current state of the industry was reported back to the House on 31 March 1712.[44] In support of the manufacturers, figures were presented which included an estimate of 21,268 families employed in the industry; reckoning three to a family, this was a total of 63,804 persons. It was claimed that £150,000 had been lost 'before the manufactures were brought to perfection', and that £45,000 had been expended in the building of various works. As a result of competition from the new home industry, the price of imported brass per cwt had dropped from £8 10s to £7 10s during the previous ten years. Elsewhere in evidence, figures were given by customs officials for brass and brassware importations for the seven years from 1703 to 10. Consisting of finished battery, metal-prepared and black lattin, the total amounted to 28,771cwt; averaging 205 tons per annum.

Arthur Thomas, one of the partners of the Bristol brass works gave evidence, and in addition to detailing the amount of pit coal used in the production of brass, explained that the two Bristol copper works used over 2,000 horse-loads of coal per week. He also stated that the different grades of brassware—battery, metal-prepared and black lattin—were equal in cost and workmanship, thus giving weight to the claim that differences in their duties should be discarded.

Much conflicting evidence was given on the quality of English-made brass, but undoubtedly opinions were prejudiced according to the side they were meant to support, the merchants or manufacturers. A detailed inspection of the more unbiased reports indicates that the early brass produced at Bristol had been variable and poor in quality; 'hard, flawy and scurfy', compared with imported metal. In consequence it was more difficult to work, but some craftsmen making use of it added that, in the previous two years, there had been a marked improvement in quality. This suggests that early difficulties with methods that were probably experimental, were begining to be overcome. The chief dealers in battery and the working braziers in Bristol produced a statement, which certified 'That the Proprietors of the Brass and Battery Works in that City have brought their Works to such Perfection, that they have been for many Years past, supplied with Battery, of their own Making, of all Sorts and Sizes, suitable to the Market, equal in all respects, and above 20s per C Weight cheaper that what they were formerly supplied with from Holland, to their own and Customers entire Satisfaction'.[45]

At the end of this exhaustive enquiry, the government decided not to grant further protection to the industry, thus leaving the Bristol company to make its own headway in home and foreign trade. For a number of years, little was heard of the controversy.

## Growth and Further Petition

At the time of the committee enquiry, Anders Swab from Sweden was investigating the progress of the English copper and brass industries. He estimated that 3,000 to 4,000 ship-pounds (400–533 tons) of refined copper was being produced in Bristol.[46] From other assessments it seems probable that the lower figure was nearer the truth, but this large production emphasised a point made in evidence to the House of Commons by Arthur Thomas, that there were two large copper works in Bristol.

The second site was at Crew's Hole, half a mile downstream from the Conham works of Elton and Wayne. It had been established by the brass company to produce a part of their requirements of refined copper, and most of its output went to Baptist Mills. Swab discovered, however, that not all copper produced in Bristol was suitable for making brass. About half of the output was forged and manufactured to be marketed as copperware.[47]

Thus, by 1712, the organisation of the Bristol brass company relied partly on production at Crew's Hole copper works. It was sited on a bend in the Avon where the river was still tidal, permitting ore brought into the port to be taken upstream of the city and unloaded on the banks of the smelting works. A short distance further upstream the Conham works received supplies in a similar way, and also disposed of most of the copper it produced to the Bristol brass works. The brass metal was smelted 2 miles away at Baptist Mills works, the production headquarters of the company where batteryware was also made. In addition, a large quantity of battery was manufactured at Keynsham.

Anders Swab found that Bristol brass was produced in twenty-five furnaces at Baptist Mills which were kept going daily, and he estimated that they used 1,500 ship-pounds (200 tons) of copper annually.[48] This figure appears to be quite feasible when compared with Arthur Thomas's evidence of 500 tons used over two years at Bristol and elsewhere in the country. It suggests that the output of brass at Baptist Mills was in the region of 250–60 tons per annum, well in excess of the import figures estimated at 205 tons.

The Bristol output more than doubled within the next few years. According to a company statement the total value of annual sales, made up of brass metal, battery and wire, in the years preceding 1720, amounted on average to £80,000.[49] At prices quoted in evidence to the parliamentary committee, brass and brassware to this value would have probably exceeded 570 tons per annum.

In September 1720, the company stated that it had 'lately entered into another coalition with proprietors of Several Great Copperworks which have hitherto served them with copper'. To make these arrangements it had been necessary to admit new proprietors to the joint-stock company and, in consequence, the original eighty shares, which in any case had already changed hands many times, were now very widely distributed. There was general concern that the company might be contravening the newly passed Bubble Act.[50] This measure, prohibiting the formation of joint-stock companies without first obtaining an Act of Incorporation, had been passed just four months earlier at the height of a financial crisis. The creation of the South Sea Company, in 1711, had given rise to the formation of several other purely speculative schemes, which came to be known collectively as the South Sea Bubble. The ease with which fortunes could be made, or were thought to be made, by capital gains, led to further outbreaks of financial speculation, particularly after 1717 until, eventually, the Bubble Act was passed as a preventive measure.

Under certain sections of the Act, companies established before

24 June 1718 could be exempted, and therefore the case of the
Bristol brassmakers went, with others in this category, before Sir
Sir Thomas Pengelley, the king's Prime Sergeant-at-Law. The
information put before him for consideration has provided a
valuable record of the earlier years of the Bristol brass company,
and of similar organisations. Of the twenty-seven projects he considered, fifteen were found to violate the Act, including Temple
Mills brassworks, the Welsh Copper Company, and two other brass
companies that were not named; but the Bristol brassmakers learned
that their enterprise would be allowed to continue.[51] Thomas Pengelley advised them against any further increase in the number of
shares, but those existing could continue to be transferred by being
recorded in the transfer book.[52] Indeed, the meticulous way in
which the company's business had been organised in its early
years greatly favoured its continued existence.

With this legal hurdle now behind them, the Bristol company
found itself in a greatly improved position, with some rival businesses declared illegal by Thomas Pengelley, and an alliance already
legally approved with the most important of the remaining companies. At this juncture, a further attempt was made to overcome
the old difficulties experienced with import duties. The mine
owners of Devon and Cornwall joined with the manufacturers in
presenting dual petitions to the House of Commons on 8 January
1722.[53] Most of the arguments were repeated from those previously
made in 1712. Again, they dwelt on the illogical way in which
brassware was divided into categories carrying different rates of
duty, but there was also an added emphasis on the competitive
prices now faced from brass imported from the continent, although
it is not clear if such imports had recently intensified.[54]

The two petitions produced an even greater number of counter-
claims than in 1712. The strength of this opposition to further
restrictions on imports of brass, gives an indication that the
English product was not yet all that could be desired. Bristol
merchants even declared their opposition to the brassmakers, re-

questing that no extra duties should be laid on Dutch brass which they re-exported to the plantations.[55]

The House of Commons again appointed an inquiry into the arguments. It reported back on 2 February 1722, with proposals which were intended to give increased protection against categories of metal-prepared and black lattin brassware, and certain types of imported ores, as requested by the mining industry. Parliament voted against the scheme, bringing failure to all the efforts to stem foreign competition.[56] But the Bristol industry was approaching the stage of technical competence when customs duties were unnecessary in combating continental imports. In later years the claim was made that 'they not only raised the Trade but were princlly Instrumental in Establishing it so Effectually that the Importation of Foreign Wrought Brass and Copper Manufactures was greatly diminished by the year 1740'.[57]

CHAPTER THREE

# *Early Techniques and Organisation*

'The principal place where English brass is made is at Baptist Mills near Bristol.'

Emanuel Swedenborg, *de Cupro* (1734)

### *The Copper Combination*

Henric Kahlmeter of the Bergskollegiet, the Swedish Board of Mines, visited England in the early 1720s with the object of gaining information. Swedish officials were concerned at the rapid progress in the techniques of this country's metallurgical industries, more particularly of the copper mines and works which were beginning to threaten the export trade of their own country. Kahlmeter formed the opinion that the copper-smelting works at Bristol, together with those at Redbrook on the other side of the Severn estuary, were the 'most considerable' in England.[1]

The companies running the four main sites he saw in these places were working together by this time in some form of trade association—the coalition to which reference was made in the case put before Sir Thomas Pengelley. On that occasion, the 'Several Great Copperworks' concerned were not identified,[2] but they emerge gradually from other contemporary references.

Several partners from different copper works had amalgamated, as adventurers, to run a group of Cornish copper mines under the direction of John Coster, junior. On 3 June 1719, an agreement was signed between Lord Falmouth as landowner, and Coster on behalf of the partners, to construct a deep adit to drain an area of North Downs near Redruth, and to search and mine for copper ore. Earlier in the century, Gabriel Wayne had mined ore for his

Conham furnaces at Wheal Varia (or Wheal Vreah) on part of North Downs, and the Coster family had had similar connections here, and at Chasewater nearby, almost from the turn of the century.[3]

The adventurers named as party to the agreement between John Coster and Lord Falmouth, included Coster's elder brother, 'Thomas Coster and Nehemiah Champion on behalf of themselves and partners; Abraham Elton on behalf of himself and Gabriel Wayne; Thomas Chambers and John Essington on behalf of themselves and the Governors and Company of Copper Miners in England'.[4] These men were representative of the four principal smelting works at Redbrook and Bristol. Thomas Coster was a proprietor of the Upper Redbrook Copper Works; Chambers and Essington of the English Copper Company of Lower Redbrook; Elton and Wayne of the Conham works, Bristol. Whilst Nehemiah Champion appears to have been associated with Thomas Coster in this agreement, probably through the Redbrook company, he was very soon taking full responsibility for the brass company's works at Bristol.

In addition to running the North Downs group of mines, members of the combination participated in the working of other sites in Devon and Cornwall, which doubtless would have become involved in the smelters' association. The brass company was concerned in the 1720s with the working of several mines in the Tavistock area: Bedford and Marquisse west of the town, and Duke, Stocklake and Virtuous Lady to the south. They also took part in the running of Tolgusdown, near Redruth, one of the oldest copper mines in Cornwall, as well as Wheal Lovely near Poldice, and Wheal Howl near Camborne. They were the sole proprietors of part of the copper-mining area at North Molton in North Devon, which was still said to yield a very rich ore. By now the carriage overland to Barnstaple cost 10s per ton, and shipping from there to Bristol or Chepstow, was 5s per ton.[5]

The association of smelters co-operated in other ways, par-

ticularly to depress ore prices from producers at other Cornish
mines. The Bristol smelters had been obtaining copper ore from
Cornwall at very low prices from the 1690s, paying as little as
£2 2s 6d to £4 per ton, because mine owners, more experienced
with tin, were not aware of its true value.[6] By the time its worth
was realised, the association of smelting companies was working
together, refusing to buy ore until prices dropped to a low level.
Men in Cornwall strongly advocated smelting their own copper
locally in the same way as they smelted tin, by legally guarded
privilege. Works were established for local smelting, but lack of
coal resources prevented any real success. Far greater quantities
of coal were needed in proportion, usually about three times as
much coal as copper ore and, in consequence, it was cheaper to
transport ore to areas where coal was easily available.[7]

Thus by 1727, John Coster, junior, was responsible for buying
large quantities of ore. Not only was he supplying the Upper Redbrook works of his family concern, but also their neighbours, the
English Copper Company in the lower part of the parish, Elton
and Wayne at Conham works, and the Crew's Hole works of the
brass company. These companies continued to receive ore purchased by John Coster until his death in 1731.[8] William Pryce in
*Mineralogia Cornubiensis*, referred to the way in which these companies were 'united and confederated'.

Meanwhile, the Coster family business, continued by the three
sons, Thomas, John and Robert after the death of John Coster,
senior, in 1718, had expanded its interests in mining, and gained
new sources of ore supplies.[9] During the 1720s, the Costers were
closely connected with the running of Hocklake and Impham mines
near Tavistock, and Frenches Work near Helston. They also had
an agreement to buy all ore produced at Relistia mine, near the
village of Gwinear, and they must have formed many other connections which were not recorded. The family was assisted in these
enterprises by several innovations which it was responsible for
introducing. The most important was 'An Engine for Drawing

*Sketches made at Warmley by Reinhold Angerstein in 1754:* (right) *the steam engine;* (below) *a reverberatory copper furnace*

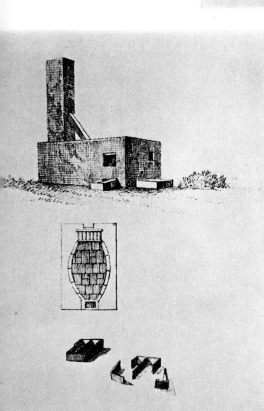

Water out of Deep Mines much Cheaper and more Effectual than the Usual Ways by Water Wheels'. This was Patent No 397, registered by John Coster, senior, together with his son John, in 1714. It claimed that the 'engine' was capable of raising a quantity of water, greater by one-third, from a depth one-third greater, than by means previously used. The details of the old methods are not recorded with any certainty, but involved using a series of small waterwheels, and these were replaced by the Costers with some new form of water-powered pump. It worked cranks from opposite sides of a wheel, which alternately raised and lowered the ends of two arms, counterweighted by balance bobs.[10] From the opposite end of the arms, chains were suspended holding pistons which moved up and down in cylinders made of brass or cast iron, providing an effective pumping system.

This kind of drainage 'engine', was probably the one installed by John Coster, junior, in 1716 at North Downs, before the agreement with the combined smelters, and is typical of the kind of improvement made by the Costers in Cornish mines. They increased the use of drainage adits, introduced the use of the horse whim into the county, and started new systems of assaying and dressing the ores.[11] Their success in these new techniques was responsible for a great improvement in the output of Cornish mines, and most of the extra production they gained found its way to Redbrook and Bristol.

BRISTOL SMELTING

In Bristol by the 1720s, the two most important copper works were almost entirely geared to the requirements of brass production and both were situated upstream of the city within easy reach of Baptist Mills.[12]

In addition, a smaller business was working on the banks of the Avon downstream of the city at Stockley Vale, probably on the old site used by the Clerkes before the turn of the century. This was started about 1720 by John Hobbs, who used ten furnaces to

D

smelt Cornish ores, producing copper to be made into brass ingots by the Bristol brass works. This indicates that the quality of copper produced was not suitable for batteryware and wire, but adequate for casting. Five years later, the works changed hands and then ceased to function, although there were plans to recover copper from the piles of slag on the river banks.

At the largest works at Conham, Elton and Wayne had thirty furnaces installed. Their whole production, which sometimes approached 200 tons per annum, was being absorbed by the brass company, but when Kahlmeter visited the works in 1725, he estimated that they were producing only half that amount from lack of ore. In addition to Cornish ores, regular quantities were received at Conham from County Wicklow in Ireland.

Kahlmeter also visited Crew's Hole, half a mile away, at the more modern works established by the Bristol brass company. He found twenty-four reverberatory furnaces there, larger and more complicated than those described by Cletscher at Conham at the start of the local industry. They were grouped together in one well-constructed building called the cupola. The main furnaces, twenty-three of them, were 5ft 6in to 6ft long and 3ft to 3ft 6in wide at the firebox, widening to about 4ft at the centre and decreasing to 1ft 2in to 2ft at the duct to the chimney. The crosswall dividing the ore bed from the firebox was 1ft 6in high, leaving an opening of 10in to allow access for the flame to reach the main chamber. The roof was vaulted, rising from the firebox and gradually decreasing to 1ft 3in or 10in, and ore was charged through an opening at the top. The ore bed was lined with sand, and other surfaces were of Stourbridge clay. Some of the furnaces had a perpendicular chimney and in others it was built obliquely through the wall of the main cupola building.[13]

By this period the process had developed from that described by Cletscher in the early days at Conham. The furnaces had first to be heated, a process which took from one to two days, meanwhile, ores were sometimes calcined in a preliminary stage. More usually, they were loaded directly in 300lb lots into the reverberatory furnaces with the addition of $\frac{3}{4}$ bushel of lime, together with silica in some form, and copper slag from previous batches of the operation. The furnaces were recharged every 4 hours and the slag was tapped every 12 hours, afterwards the copper matte was tapped into oblong moulds hollowed out in a sand bed.

When solidified, the copper matte was broken into pieces and reloaded into the furnace to be roasted in a moderate heat for 12 to 14 hours, using a fuel consisting of one-third of coal to two-thirds coke. During this time the charge was not allowed to melt, but subsequently, the heat was increased for a period of 2 to 3 hours to melt the matte, which was then tapped into sand moulds as before. This operation was repeated from ten to twenty times, according to the quality of the matte.

The smelting processes were completed in the one refining furnace, which was similar to those previously used, apart from being narrower, and it was built into the same cupola construction. A layer of bone ash called slough, 2 to 3in thick, covered the bed of the ore hearth and the first, or coarse stage, of refining lasted 12 to 16 hours, with only coal as fuel. The melted mass was tested by colour and fracture from samples in a small iron ladle. The second, fine refining, heated with charcoal, lasted only 2 hours. The melt was over-oxidised and reduced back with charcoal, then sulphur was added to reduce the cuprous oxide content. The quality of copper thus produced was suitable for making the highest grades of brass to manufacture wire and batteryware.[14]

The Cornish ores normally used in the Bristol smelting works often contained appreciable quantities of tin, causing a high-tin bronze to liquate to the bottom of the refining furnace. This was sold to founders for the production of bell metal, there being several well-known bellfounders within the surrounding area. Small quantities of ore were received at Crew's Hole works from West New Jersey, new York, amounting to some 50 tons during 1724. The arrival of a further 80 tons was anticipated in the following year.

Previously, Crew's Hole had been known to produce up to 200 tons of copper per annum, when ore was more easily obtained. At the time of Kahlmeter's report in 1725, he estimated the total output to be about 150 tons, most of which was intended for brass.

The lower grades of local coal, adequate for fuelling the copper furnaces were delivered to the smelting works for 6d per seam, inclusive of 3d per seam for carriage. A seam should have equalled 300lb but was commonly only 250lb; eight seams were taken to equal 1 ton, and ten seams were usually required every twenty-four hours for each copper furnace. Thirty-three men were employed at Crew's Hole, and paid regularly at a rate of 6s per week, regardless of periods when there was no work through lack of ore supplies.

Market prices for refined copper in Bristol at the beginning of 1725 were: best grades for brass battery, £5 15s to £6 per cwt; best grades for copper battery, £5 10s to £5 15s per cwt.[15]

## COPPER-BATTERY WORKS

Another development in the Bristol industry was brought about by the Coster family, as a part of the family business which had no direct connection with the Bristol brass works, or the Upper Redbrook Copperworks Company. John Coster, senior, had been involved in the Redbrook smelting works from the close of the previous century, in a partnership of proprietors from outside his family. He continued to be concerned with the site, producing copper of high quality but, in 1708, he also took over the lease of an old fulling-mill at Swinford, on the Avon, about two miles upstream from the brass-mill at Keynsham. Coster converted the mill at Swinford to roll sheet copper, keeping the business separate from Redbrook with the partners confined only to his family. The deeds of these premises record the first known instance in the area of this method of fabricating sheet metal.[16]

By 1713, the family had leased another mill in the Bristol area, in the name of the eldest son, Thomas. Eight miles to the south on the River Chew, another tributary of the Avon, this new site was at Bye Mills, where already there existed a long history of iron-battery work.[17] The Costers adapted the premises to continue this function in a revised form, producing copper batteryware from sheet rolled at the Swinford Mill.

In later years, after the business had been taken over by the three sons at the death of their father in 1718, another mill on the River Chew, near Publow Church, was taken over and adapted for rolling and battery work and at one period, some refining was carried out here. Yet another mill lying between Bye Mills and Publow, at Pensford, was also leased by the Costers, but continued its work as a grist mill. Its mill house was converted for use as a warehouse for copper goods, but the mill was never adapted. Possibly, it had been desirable to obtain the lease for the purpose of holding the water rights, or for navigation between the copper mills.[18]

By 1727, copper battery to the value of £15,000 was being sold annually at Bristol, and probably the largest part was being produced at the mills belonging to the Coster family. The business continued to expand successfully, although it was a rival concern to the Bristol brass company to some extent. It has often been assumed that the Costers were also partners of the brass company, but as staunch members of the Church of England it seems unlikely that they would have associated closely with such a strong Quaker organisation. John Coster, senior, left no shares of the brass company in his will, but there may have been some business connection through Thomas Coster, the eldest son who lived in Bristol and became the city's member of parliament. The Coster family business does also appear to have provided some kind of service to all the associated smelting companies.[19]

## The Bristol Brass Company

### NEHEMIAH CHAMPION AND BAPTIST MILLS

Early in the 1720s, Nehemiah Champion was providing leadership for the Bristol brass company. It is possible that he may have held this responsibility from the time that Abraham Darby relinquished the role, but no information has been discovered on management in the intervening years.

Champion came from a family already concerned with many aspects of the metal industries. His father (also Nehemiah) was a Bristol merchant who achieved a special relationship in his trading with Darby's Coalbrookdale works. Nehemiah, the son, carried on this trade as his father became more elderly and Richard, the younger son, also a successful Bristol merchant, had provided financial assistance to Abraham Darby at Coalbrookdale for a short term in 1712.[20]

Prior to this time, there had been a William Champion involved in the application for a charter of a projected 'Company for the Digging and Working of Mines' in 1693, and a John Champion is recorded in the Neath Port Books as the consignee of copper ores from Cornwall on many occasions from 1695.[21] Connections have not been discovered between these two men and the Quaker Champions of Bristol, but there is no doubt of the Bristol family's interest in metallurgical concerns.

Whether Nehemiah junior was in charge of the Bristol brass company when his name appeared on the Cornish mining agreement of 1719 (page 49) is unfortunately not recorded but, by 1723, Champion was in possession of Patent No 454, relating to techniques developed and used at the Bristol brass works. The first part of the patent specification concerned the preparation of copper for brassmaking, and was to have a permanent effect on the method of making calamine brass. It was entitled

A Method of converting Copper into Brass by a New Way of preparing the Copper to receive a much greater Proporčon of Calamy, and making a much greater Increase of Brass from the Copper and Calamy that have hitherto been done, and to make the Copper and Calamy into Brass in much less Time and Expense than has been done by any Method before practised.[22]

The improvement referred to in the specification was based on the granulation of copper. In this form copper was more easily per-meated by the zinc vapour which was produced from calamine during the brassmaking process. This was hardly apparent from the vague description of the patent which vainly tried to keep the process secret; but just two years after its registration, Henric Kahlmeter described the method in detail in information which was sent back to Sweden.[23]

He had been entertained by Nehemiah Champion at Bristol, and part of the works was shown to him but it is evident that he discovered more than was intended.[24] From his account, it can be learned that attempts had been made originally at Baptist Mills to granulate the metal by simply pouring it into an open vessel con-taining a supply of water, but this was abandoned as too dangerous. Subsequently, an improved container was devised which consisted of a wooden receptacle, 4 to 5ft deep, with a false bottom of brass or copper which could be raised or lowered by means of chains. It was covered with a lid, and had a 6in diameter hole in the centre, with raised sides which held a removable ladle pierced with holes.

The ladle was protected with Stourbridge clay to withstand the heat of molten copper being poured through it, which separated out into large granules as it fell through cold running water to the bottom of the vessel. Early experiments had failed because the container only held a static water supply. This became heated as the molten copper dropped into it so preventing granulation, as the metal spread out into thin plates. When the vessel was adapted to receive a constant flow of cold water, the temperature was kept low enough for the granules to solidify. They were then raised to the surface of the vessel by lifting the false bottom by the chains.[25]

This method of copper granulation was almost certainly adapted from the process of making lead shot, which was carried out in the Bristol area. In the 1690s, John Houghton referred to Bristol goose-shot, and described the method of making it; a very similar operation to Champion's patented process for copper granulation.[26]

Champion's brassmaking process at Baptist Mills which utilised the copper granules, required the addition of calcined calamine in the same way as the old method. The traditional method of preparing calamine had been described in detail by Giles Pooley of Wrington, at the request of the president of the Royal Society, in 1684.[27] At that time, Mendip ore was being sent abroad to Holland for making brass, in the absence of a local market. By the 1720s England was importing calamine from Aix-la-Chapelle, in the brass-making area of the German–Dutch borders, and Mendip ores, fully prepared by the Mendip miners, were being sent direct to Baptist Mills. First the calamine was carefully cleansed by them and any lead particles were separated by handpicking. It was then washed in buddles, and further separated by shaking through a sieve, a process known as jigging. The ore was then crushed by horse-propelled edgerunners, or vertical millstones, a great improvement from the days of Pooley, when men had crushed the ore with hammers. Otherwise the method of preparing the ore was much the same as in his period.

When the calamine was ground to a powder it was loaded into wood-burning reverberatory furnaces, in 4 to 5in layers to be calcined for about six hours and turned at intervals with long-handled rakes. By the end of the period, the substance was completely converted from zinc carbonate to a zinc oxide suitable for brassmaking. It had also been changed to a lumpy consistency, which had to be crushed to a powder again under the horse-powered edgerunners. The material was then taken by horse transport to the brass works at Baptist Mills.[28] The works there may have also received small amounts of calamine from mines which had been projected earlier in the century, at Durdham Down on the northern side of Avon Gorge, quite close to the centre of Bristol.

At Baptist Mills in the early 1720s, Kahlmeter reported thirty-six furnaces for making brass, the works which Swedenborg described some ten years later as 'the principal place where English brass is made'. The furnaces were built into six separate brass-houses but not all were kept going continuously to produce the annual output which was estimated at 300 tons of brass. From his brief description, which is all that is available for this early period, it seems quite clear that the method was basically similar to that employed in the previous century. Eight crucibles made of Stour-bridge clay were inserted into each circular furnace and emptied twice every twenty-four hours.[29]

The main development appears to have taken place in the outer structure of the furnace housing. In seventeenth-century descriptions of furnaces in England, and in those of continental furnaces until quite late in the eighteenth century, no provision appears to be made for any special kind of chimney. In contrast, a distant view of Baptist Mills in the 1730s shows several large cones at the brass works, similar to the glass cones of Bristol.[30] Thus, it seems probable that each one of the six brass houses described by Kahl-meter would have contained six furnaces built into a cone structure, in the same way as the brass houses seen by Hatchett in Birming-ham at the end of the eighteenth century.[31] The new kind of structure may have been developed to provide additional draught for the coal fuel of the brassmaking process at Bristol.

Even after the introduction of Champion's granulated-copper process, the old method of making brass with broken copper was still employed at Baptist Mills. The two processes were otherwise similar, but the brass produced showed important differences. Using broken copper, it was said that the works made 56lb brass from every 40lb copper, after adding 56 to 60lb calamine.[32] This increase in weight over and above the amount of copper employed, represented the weight of zinc plus a small amount of impurities, absorbed to form the alloy. It was the basis of the brassmakers' art, although it was far from being understood at the time. In 1697, only some twenty-five years before, John Houghton had described calamine as 'A sort of stone that will give to copper both weight and colour, and thus brass is made'. It was a typical description, not recognising that calamine was a metalliferous ore containing zinc, or that zinc was a metal which alloyed with copper in the process of brass manufacture. At the time, metallic zinc was imported from the East into Europe in fairly small quantities, described as being mainly for the preparation of solders, but no one connected this imported metal with brassmakers' calamine.[33] By the days of Champion's ascendancy in the Bristol brass company, a greater understanding was beginning to evolve.

Much of the zinc in calamine was inevitably lost in the brassmaking process, owing to the difficulty of handling a substance which volatilised so easily. Copper was by far the more costly of the two constituents of brass, but the less zinc lost, the more brass was produced from the same quantity of copper. Thus the skilled brassmaker of the early eighteenth century tried to increase the weight of copper by absorbing as much calamine as possible. If the works at Baptist Mills was actually achieving the increase claimed when making use of broken copper, it appears to have been more successful than many manufacturers of its time. Possibly the Mendip calamine was of better quality than that employed in many continental works. In modern terms Baptist Mills appears to have produced a brass of 72 per cent copper, to 28 per cent zinc inclusive of any impurities present.

After the introduction of granulated copper to the process, Kahlmeter found that the works was producing brass with an increase of 50 per cent on the weight of copper used. This represents a brass that today would be described as $66\frac{2}{3}$ per cent copper to $33\frac{1}{3}$ per cent zinc,[34] and was approaching the most economical type of brass capable of being used in the Bristol company's processes. Theoretically, it contains too much zinc for the best grade of battery work and wire but this excess is marginal in practice. Thus the ability to produce this grade of metal must have contributed greatly to the success of the company.

The technical improvements brought about at Baptist Mills in this period were probably developed in the laboratory attached to the works, where experimental methods of converting copper to brass were carried out within a building containing several kinds of furnaces.[35] The new annealing furnace, which appeared in the second part of Champion's Patent No 454 in 1723, would undoubtedly have been developed there. This provided 'A New Way of Nealing the Plates and Kettles with Pitt Cole, which softens and makes the Brass as Tough and Fine-coloured as any nealed with Wood and Wood-cole'. As described by Kahlmeter, the interior dimensions of this furnace were 5ft square by 4ft high with an arched roof and side walls 1ft 6in thick. It held cast-iron containers, 3 to 4ft long by 2ft wide, which were mounted on wheels and could be conveyed mechanically into place in the oven. The brass vessels to be annealed were nested into one another and placed in the containers, which were then sealed with clay to prevent fumes from the coal spoiling the brass. The door of the furnace was raised by a chain and probably counter-balanced in a similar way to the later annealing furnaces (plate, page 88).

The laboratory at Baptist Mills contained other equipment in addition to the various furnaces, but unfortunately the descriptions are vague. There were several types of water-powered machines including a small hammer for testing the number of blows a piece of brass could withstand. There were other methods of striking the metal at various points with teeth, and machines were installed which were capable of cutting and flattening brass.[36] This works laboratory appears to have contained some of the earliest known equipment in England, used in the science of materials testing.

ORGANISATION OF NEW SITES

In addition to progress in the techniques of making brass and the attendant smelting of copper, the 1720s brought a period of expansion in the organisation of mill sites along the River Avon.

In 1721, the Bristol brass company leased land at Saltford, about four miles above their mill at Keynsham and erected 'copperworks'.[37] These works were never comparable with the copper-smelting sites lower down the Avon, near Bristol. The remains which survive today are of the Old Brass Mills and they were, undoubtedly, established as battery mills, equally suitable for working up sheets of brass or copper into hollow-ware by the battery process.

A few years later, another brass-battery mill owned by the company is known to have been in existence, further upstream in the parish of Weston, about one and a half miles west of Bath. Entries of foreign workers appear from 1723 in the registers of Twerton parish church on the south bank of the river. These include John Jockman, a Dutchman buried in 1723; George, son of John and Elizabeth (no surname), Dutchman, baptised in 1724; and a burial recorded later for the Buik or Buick family which may be connected with the Bucks, the brassworkers recorded at Keynsham.[38] There are several entries for the Graft, Graff or Graef family, described as Dutch, although a stone memorial in the church indicates their home was in Veit in Germany, thus confirming that some workers described as Dutch had origins in various parts of the Low Countries.

The dating of these family records suggests that the mill at Weston may have been almost contemporary with the establishing of Saltford Mills in 1721. More reliable evidence can be traced by 1729, in a plan which shows that the mill was by then definitely working. This is attached to deeds of property sold by the proprietors of the Avon Navigation.[39]

A channel cut in 1727 on the north bank, bypassed the weirs at the Weston and Twerton mills, and was one of the final tasks in the work of making the Avon navigable from Bath to Hanham Mills where tidal waters provided a passage through to the Bristol Channel. The scheme had been projected in March 1725 by John Hobbs, owner of the copper works started in Stockley Vale, but better known as a timber merchant. Among the thirty-two shareholders of the Avon Navigation Company were John Hobbs himself, and Dr John Lane, copper smelter of Swansea, who may have been connected with the brass works in some capacity (page 74). More famous was Ralph Allen of Bath, postmaster of the city, who was destined to become a wealthy man by exploitation of the local Bath stone.[40]

In December 1727, the river was fully opened to Bath, with all mill weirs bypassed by locks. At Weston, the cutting of the new channel left the brass mill on an island, Dutch Island, as it was to become known locally. A small stone footbridge was built by the navigation company to allow access to the brass company property, and a coloured drawing of it, entitled 'A View of Twiverton near Bath', is believed to be a preliminary sketch of a painting which belonged to Ralph Allen. The drawing, now in the map-room of the British Museum, shows the canal bridge at Weston with steps leading to it, very much as they do today. A building partly hidden by trees has a large square chimney pouring out smoke; the annealing chimney of the brass works.[41]

With the opening of the navigation, the various sites of the brass company became more accessible to one another, with the exception of Baptist Mills. The watermills had predominance in their legal right to use river water, and when water was low, barges were often held up because locks were closed to conserve water. The busy brass mills were often blamed for delays in river transport, but the existence of the navigation must have been a great advantage to the brass company and it is probably from this period that Baptist Mills began to decline in importance within the organisation. It was gradually replaced by Avon Mill on the main river route at Keynsham.

The wire-mill was developed here, producing one of the two principal end-products in the long chain of processes which the company undertook. There are several references in Keynsham church registers to wireworkers by the 1740s. Surprisingly, there are also records, in this same period, of men who worked at the cupiloes. These are later explained by an account of a visit to Keynsham by Dr Richard Pococke who stated, 'there, near the church are some houses for smelting copper'.[42] The reverberatory furnaces for copper smelting were often described as cupiloes in the area surrounding Bristol. Those at Keynsham must have been sited on the triangle of ground at the confluence of the tributary River Chew with the Avon. Later, references occur to a cinder heap near this point, which would have consisted of waste slag from the smelting furnaces, but it seems unlikely that this process was ever carried out on a large scale at Keynsham.

Another mill in the village was developed to produce battery-ware and was working by mid-century, possibly long before.[43] This was Chew Mill, the lowest site on the River Chew, quite close to Avon Mill. Thus, in years approaching the mid-century, most of the stages of brass manufacture carried out by the company were being undertaken in Keynsham.

The resulting influx of workers caused difficulty in the administration of the parish poor rate, as the village was still quite small. Many of the skilled workers brought from the Low Countries could not return home if they fell on hard times through ill-health or other misfortune. In such circumstances, English workers would have been sent back to 'their place of settlement', under the Act of 1662. There were several disputes between the paymaster of the parish of Keynsham and the proprietors of the brass company, which eventually led to an 'Agreement made between the Parish of Keynsham and the Brass Wire Work Company concerning the men and their families', signed 30 June 1740. This clarified several points which had caused mutual dissatisfaction, but mainly involved the relief of those workers and their families who could not return home, should they fall in need of financial assistance.

The company agreed, in future, to take responsibility for workers and their families in this category. They were also to take a parish apprentice and to provide him with the usual food, lodging and laundry (in addition to the trade apprentices which the company normally took). The first boy nominated by the agreement was the son of the late widow Rawlins, of an old Keynsham family, but another boy was to be accepted three years later. Finally, the proprietors agreed to pay the cost of the agreement and to provide 2gns for distribution to the poor the following Easter, to celebrate the ending of the dispute.[44]

The foreign workers at Keynsham by then included such names as Ollis, Frankham, Steger and Craymer, and possibly also Buck and Racker, who can all be traced in parish registers, with variable spelling and the remark 'no parishioner' often added. No early record can be found of other names which are connected by tradition with the works, such as Crinks, Fudge and Hollister. Possibly they came to Keynsham at a later date, from other premises of the company. A comparative latecomer, John Varoy, apprenticed his son to the company as a wiredrawer in 1745.[45] His name was later anglicised to Fray and the family joined the foreign workers who continued to work at the mills until the local industry came to an end. This tendency was apparently encouraged by the company, which was said to guarantee employment for the third or fourth generation of workers from the continent.[46]

The industry was still developing at places other than Keynsham. Further to the south, on the River Chew near Compton Dando, Woodborough Mill was leased by the company and adapted as a battery-mill during the 1730s.[47] It had been a mill from at least the 1590s, and was owned by the Popham family, as were the nearby copper mills leased by the Costers.

DEVELOPMENTS IN SMELTING

Thomas Coster, eldest of the three brothers, was elected Member of Parliament for Bristol during 1734, three years after the death of his brother John of Cornwall. During 1734 a new partner was taken into the family business, Joseph Percival, who purchased a third share in the company.[48] In the ensuing year Robert Coster, the youngest of the brothers, died, followed by Thomas in 1739 at the age of 54. His monument can still be seen in Bristol Cathedral.

There were no male heirs to take over the business and Thomas's only daughter, Jane, married to Robert Hoblyn, MP, had the controlling interest for some years. Eventually this was completely transferred to Joseph Percival, who changed the name of the business to Joseph Percival & Copper Company and took several new partners. Later he expanded the works, particularly at a new copper-smelting site at White Rock, near Swansea, which had been established in 1737 in the name of Jane Hoblyn. This site was to become one of the principal smelting works of its area during the eighteenth century. From here, large quantities of refined copper were sent to Bristol to be fabricated at the mills of Swinford, Bye Mills and Publow.

The Bristol brass company could have been hard hit by the loss of John Coster, junior, in supplying copper ore from Cornwall, had not a regular system for sales been organised at about the time of his death. This was brought about by the intervention of a new manufacturer from Swansea, Robert Morris, who had taken over the bankrupted business of his former employer, John Lane. Not being included in the smelters' association, Morris offered the mine owners far better prices, £6 5s per ton, as against £4 5s, which was all the combination would pay. This precipitated a new agreement between smelters and mine owners, by which all ore supplies were sold by public 'ticketed' sales. At an appointed time and place, smelters' agents assembled and handed in a ticket for each lot of ore to be sold, carrying the price tendered, with the name of the company, and the lot was passed to the highest bidder.[49] The system was still favourable to the smelters, who continued to force prices down by mutual agreement.

In addition, the Bristol brass company still had another means of supply at this period, from the mines which they entirely owned and which sent their ores direct to Bristol.[50]

From about the early 1730s the Bristol brass company took over the lease of the Upper Redbrook copper works. Viscount Gage, the landowner, later declared that 'It afterwards appeared that [the

Page 69 *At Warmley:* (above) *the row of cottages believed to have been built by William Champion were demolished in quite recent years;* (below) *the clock-tower building was also to go, but was reprieved at the last moment*

Page 70 (above) *The Old Brass Mills, Saltford, are now deteriorating rapidly;* (below) *the remains of the battery mill at Keynsham are incorporated in the Memorial Park*

company] took the works with no other view than to Ruin and Destroy them, they being in great Repute, and by that means bring the s^d trade from there to their own Works at Bristol.' He took legal action in a bid to have his property restored and, from evidence, it appears that the brass-company proprietors removed some equipment to install at Bristol.[51] Probably the Redbrook works was outdated compared with methods used at Bristol, and this may have been the reason why the site was of no further use. The name of Redbrook, however, was incorporated into the title of the brass company which then became 'The United Brass Battery, Wire and Copper Company of Bristol, Esher, Upper Redbrook and Barton Regis'. Barton Regis was an old manor and hundred of Bristol.

A more productive addition to the brass-company smelting premises was made in the Bristol area. For many years there had been a close liaison between the company and the Conham works of Elton & Wayne. When the first Sir Abraham Elton, a devout Unitarian, died in 1728, he left £10 per annum towards the support of a minister to attend the meeting-house he had provided for his workmen at Conham. He was followed by Sir Abraham II, who died in 1742, and Sir Abraham III, who was declared bankrupt in 1745. By the 1750s, the brass company had taken over the lease of the property, and continued to provide £10 annually towards the men's meeting-house, through a clause in the deeds of property which still functioned until the close of the century.[52]

The brass company began to rebuild the smelting furnaces so that, when Reinhold Angerstein visited Bristol in 1754, he saw seventeen furnaces at the new works at Conham. By this date there were forty-nine furnaces at the Crew's Hole premises, making sixty-six furnaces being operated by the brass works for smelting copper.[53] In 1749, the company had been in trouble with Bristol authorities for depositing cinder (or slag) on the banks of the river. The Report of River Nuisances noted 'A great quantity of Cinders laid upon the Banks of the said River by the Brass Wire Company

E

being a very great nuisance and likely to choak up the said river if not removed'.[54] The problems caused by the disposal of this waste material may have been a factor in persuading the company eventually to cast slag into moulds to produce building blocks. These can still be seen in the city and its surroundings, and their presence in places bordering the Severn, Avon and Wye, indicates that they were probably used as ballast for river and coastal transport.

### THE GREAT BRASS COMPANY

Angerstein visited many of the company's premises in the area between Bath and Bristol on the Avon and its tributaries, but one important site omitted was the brass warehouse in the centre of Bristol. This was located on the banks of the river, conveniently situated for shipping in the port and for barges on the Avon navigation. The building backed on to old Queen's Street, near St Phillips Church, and was included by Rocque in his plan of the city drawn in the early 1740s.[55]

Its existence accounts for the company being known as the Brass Warehouse Company, particularly in Swansea. A more familiar name to local people at this period was the Brass Wire Company, or merely BWCo, just another of the long list of titles attached to the company during its history. At Angerstein's visit to Bristol, he referred to the works quite simply as 'the Great Brass Co'.[56]

By mid-century, however, the business was not the only concern in the brass industry of Bristol. A rival company, headed by William Champion, had been formed on the outskirts of the city, and was to be developed as 'the most up-to-date and most efficient works in the country'.[57]

# CHAPTER FOUR

# William Champion and the Warmley Company

'The Warmley Works, where "the whole process of the copper and brass manufacture was exhibited from the smelting of ore to the forming it into plates, wire, pans, vessels, pins, etc.," was probably the most up-to-date and most efficient works in the country.'

Henry Hamilton, *The English Brass and Copper Industries* (1926)

THE brass works at Bristol was developed in an atmosphere of experiment and technical innovation, which continued after Darby withdrew into the period when Nehemiah Champion assumed the leadership of the company. This was the time when Champion's three sons were growing up and the eldest son, John, and the youngest, William, were both to contribute several new processes in connection with the brassmaking industry.

According to his own account, William travelled the manufacturing areas of Europe to improve his knowledge when quite a young man. He was only 20 when he returned to Bristol in 1730, and immediately set to work on a series of experiments with the aim of producing metallic zinc from ores found in England.[1] Undoubtedly Champion's interest had been stimulated by his travels, for at the time continental scholars working with metals were beginning to realise that calamine must be an ore of zinc.[2]

In England zinc, as mentioned earlier, could only be obtained by importing it from the East, where it was produced by very small-scale processes and then brought to this country under the name of tutenag or spelter. Sold in small amounts, at very high prices, it was used to make solders, and also the grades of brasses which, today, are known as gilding metals. These contain higher

73

proportions of copper to zinc than brass normally required for industrial purposes, and have a fine colour in consequence. As such, these metals could be employed to counterfeit gold, or under names such as pinchbeck or Prince's metal, could be manufactured into 'toys', or small metal articles such as button or buckles and the less expensive kinds of jewellery.[3]

Champion felt that it would be of great advantage to be able to produce zinc, or spelter as it became known, in this country. The laboratory facilities and skills of the men at his father's works must have provided him with an ideal opportunity for carrying out the work and experiment which lay ahead of him.

### Pioneer of Commercial Zinc Smelting

Zinc had actually been produced in small amounts for local consumption, at Goslar in Germany, for over a hundred years. It was was recovered intermittently as a byproduct, from the condensed gases of lead-smelting furnaces, but some confusion existed about the nature of the material being recovered.[4] Amongst other claims and experiments by continental scholars, Henckel, a German writer, stated in 1721 that he had succeeded in making zinc but no developments had arisen from his work.

At the same time, a Dr John Lane is believed to have also been experimenting at the works at Llangefelach, near Swansea, established by him in 1717, and which produced copper, lead and other metals. But he was also concerned in other ventures and subsequently was ruined by the financial disaster of the South Sea Bubble. After Lane was declared bankrupt, a former employee, Robert Morris, took over the premises and created a successful company. Morris later left papers which referred to Lane being involved in the making of spelter, but again, there were no developments.[5] The doctor, however, was a Bristol man and had associated, at least briefly, with partners of the Bristol brass company.[6] It is possible that William Champion gathered ideas or inspiration from

Lane to add to his experience gained whilst travelling in Europe.

The barrier preventing the production of zinc arose from the difficulty of creating anything of a metallic nature by heating the zinc ore, calamine. This is because it is volatile at a temperature just over 900° C, high enough for effective reduction and the production of zinc metal. Some scholars had been confused to find that vapour rising from heated calamine oxidised on contact with air, leaving them with a powdery material. Although several theories had been advanced and some accounts suggested that the problem had been solved, these solutions had been achieved by men working in laboratory conditions. William Champion was the first man to evolve a large-scale process for the commercial production of zinc.[7]

Success did not come quickly to him, and his works entailed 'great expense, study and application', for six years before he overcame the principal difficulties.[8] At the end of this period Champion was ready for his process to be patented. His specification, No 564, was entitled, 'A method of Invention for the Reducing of Sulphurous British Mineralls into a Body of Metallick Sulphur', and was granted patent rights in July 1738, for the usual term of fourteen years.

The title conveys nothing of the new process which had been developed, and no further details can be learned by reading the specification itself. It was left to Dr Watson to describe the process almost twenty years after he first saw the furnaces in operation, a delay which was almost certainly at Champion's request. Eventually, in 1766, Watson wrote:

In a circular kind of oven, like a glass-house furnace, there were placed six pots about four feet each in height, much resembling large oil jars in shape; into the bottom of each pot was inserted an iron tube, which passed through the floor of the furnace into a vessel of water. The pots were filled with a mixture of calamine and charcoal, and the mouth of each was then close stopped with clay. The fire being properly applied, the metallic vapour of the calamine issued through an iron tube, there being no other place through which it could escape, and the air being excluded, it did not take fire, but was condensed in small particles in the water, and being remelted, was formed into ingots, and sent to Birmingham under the name of zinc or spelter.[9]

This then, was William Champion's pioneering method of processing calamine to produce metallic zinc. He had solved the problems inherent in the physical properties of the metal by a process of distillation—'distillation per descensum', as it was to become known. This referred to the condensation of the zinc vapour as it descended in the iron tube through the floor of the furnace to a vessel of water in the chamber below.

Although no contemporary description of the process survives, the furnace itself was probably similar to that described by Mosselman in 1825, after visiting zinc works in England. It was circular, with a domed roof, and there were openings, through which the pots could be changed and furnace gases could escape to the large conical chimney about 30ft high.[10] The six pots containing the ore were described as 3ft 6in high, 3ft diameter across the top with a charging hole of 9in, 2ft 2in at the bottom with a hole of 6in diameter giving access to the condensing tube. Each condenser consisted of two lengths of iron tube; the flange of the upper length was pressed up against the pot by a pair of rods clamped into position; the lower length fitted over the upper, and extended down into the collecting pan. The pans were so arranged, over apertures in the floor of the furnace, that the tubes descended, three either side of a passage across the lower chamber, or cave. The upper part of this passage contained the fire grate, with space for the ash to fall into the opening below. In the two compartments containing the tubes, either side of the passage, the zinc metal was collected from the condensers and collecting pans at the end of the process, to be remelted and cast into ingots.

By preventing access of atmospheric air in his process, Champion had surmounted the difficulties of previous attempts by what today seems a comparatively simple solution. Thus, he laid foundations which were to establish an important industry, later to develop as a separate entity from copper and brass production in Bristol. His methods of making zinc, and furnaces he devised, were to remain in production for over one hundred years in Great Britain.[11]

*His Early Setbacks in Bristol*

Before this new industry could be firmly established, there were further obstacles to be overcome. As soon as patent rights had been acquired, William Champion erected large new buildings with the aim of satisfying the total demand for zinc in this country. He actually produced about 200 tons of the metal at these new premises, which apparently were situated at Baber's Tower in Back Lane, now Jacob Street just off Old Market. In September 1742, just four years after the date of his patent, Champion received complaints from the city fathers when Baber's Tower works were reported to a council meeting for causing a common nuisance. No details of the kind of trouble were mentioned in the minutes of the council meeting but, in his reply, Champion admitted that he had purchased Baber's Tower some years previously and had erected large 'fireworks' there at great expense. He had not realised that they would be a nuisance to the neighbourhood, but now they were destroyed and big improvements were planned for the site.[12]

The loss of his premises at such a vital point in production must have been a blow, but in addition to this initial setback, his difficulties were about to be aggravated by commercial problems. When the merchants importing spelter from traditional countries in the East saw that Champion could soon be making home supplies of the metal available, they realised they were liable to lose their trade, and promptly retaliated by lowering prices so drastically that the peak of £280 per ton in 1731 was reduced to £48 per ton. According to Champion's own estimate, the merchants were losing some £22 to £25 per ton by selling at these lower prices in an attempt to force him out of business. As a result he found it impossible to sell his own stocks at a price which would bring him any profit.[13]

Against this difficult background, William Champion was making plans for his large new works to be built at Warmley, 5 miles from the centre of Bristol. From the outset the premises were to be organised as a complete unit where all processes would be carried out on one site in a neighbourhood where plenty of coal was available. Copper was to be smelted and brass made, wares were to be manufactured from both these metals, all in addition to the new process of producing zinc. This was in direct contrast to similar companies of the time, particularly the old Bristol company which smelted copper at Crew's Hole, made brass at Baptist Mills, and produced goods from these metals at various points along the River Avon and its tributaries.

## The Warmley Works

### WILLIAM CHAMPION & CO, 1746–61

The new company of William Champion & Co was established in 1746, a partnership drawn from some of the members of the old Bristol company. Until then, Champion had himself been employed by the old firm, but was dismissed with a certain amount of bad feeling which greatly increased over the years.[14]

By 1748, the year Champion was first listed as a buyer of Cornish copper ores, the Warmley site was in production.[15] In October, Thomas Collinson wrote an account of his visit there which was later published in the *Gentleman's Magazine*. He saw copper ore being smelted in nineteen separate furnace operations. It was granulated in the final process in order to manufacture brass, by using similar techniques to those which William's father had patented some fifteen years previously. Calamine brass was being made and cast into long moulds made of granite slabs, producing plates of metal 4ft by 2ft by $\frac{1}{4}$in. These were slit lengthways into six or seven pieces and the resulting bars cut again into rods $\frac{1}{4}$in square on the slitting-mill, finally to be drawn into wire of various dimensions.[16]

No reference to the production of spelter was included in this early description of Collinson's, but this was almost certainly because of the secrecy which surrounded the process. By 1750, Champion was anxious for the future of his patent which was shortly due to expire. In February of that year, he petitioned the House of Commons for some form of recompense in return for his losses in bringing this new industry to the country. He pleaded particularly for an extension of the fourteen-year term of monopoly rights granted by his patent, and cited his financial difficulties brought about by the merchants' drastic lowering of prices. To substantiate his case, he drew attention to several points, including the fact that home-produced spelter was profitable to the country. It could also be supplied to industries on far more moderate terms than those previously demanded, and further, its production employed many hundreds of poor people.[17]

The following month, when a committee reported back to the House as directed, the members confirmed all of the various claims made by Champion. They added that he had expended £7,000 in producing his initial 200 tons of spelter and had suffered a loss of nearly £4,000, arising mainly from the fall in its price. A certificate was produced from several vendors and consumers, stating that for some years past they had sold and used considerable quantities of spelter made by Champion. They had found it as good as imported stocks, in some cases preferable. Birmingham and Wolverhampton were particularly mentioned as areas where large quantities had been used with complete satisfaction. The committee also reported that imports of the metal from Eastern countries had come to a halt owing to the large financial losses suffered by the merchants on their last supplies from these sources. On the whole it appeared to the members that the industry was a useful addition to the manufactures of Great Britain, consequently they ordered that leave should be granted to bring a bill for the extension of Champion's term of patent.[18]

This decision brought a counter petition from merchants and

traders. They objected on the grounds that the patentee had already had ample recompense for his discovery, that monopolies in general had a harmful and dangerous tendency, that the manufacture of brass, copper, Prince's metal, and Bath metal would be affected, and that there were already many others who were well acquainted with the mystery or secret of making spelter.[19] Some of these objections were possibly influenced by the Bristol brass company, but no reference to its name appears in the official petition. Undoubtedly members of the old company were pleased at the result; the Bill for Champion's extension of patent was subsequently abandoned.

The Warmley works does not appear to have been greatly affected by this setback, for premises at the site were in the process of being expanded. To make this possible, William Champion had installed a steam engine to supplement the power of his watermills. Apart from the actual production of metals, when the ores had been smelted and the metals poured the remaining fabrication processes needed readily available rotative power. At the time, this could only be produced reliably by waterwheels, and the small flow of Warmley Brook would have been a severe disadvantage, had there not been some means of augmenting it.

A heavy dam was constructed at the rear of the works with gates to regulate the supply of water, so creating a large pond of 13 acres. The tail water flowing from the waterwheels was then raised three fathoms (18ft) by the steam engine, and directed back into the pond, 'the water buoyed up by several tubes in a hemisphere of a conical form, falling into a pool as a cascade and affording a grand and beautiful scene'.[20]

A similar installation, augmenting rotative power by means of a steam engine capable only of pumping water, had been carried out some seven years earlier at the iron works at Coalbrookdale. The Warmley engine is believed to be an early example of this kind of combination of steam and water power which, it has been suggested, Nehemiah Champion may have played a part in developing through his patent No 567 of 1739 referring to overshot wheels.[21] In any case the Champion family would have been familiar with the Coalbrookdale engine through their business connections, and would also have known many pumping engines in the copper mines of Cornwall.

The steam engine at Warmley was considered important enough to merit a report in the *Bristol Journal*, 13 September 1749, just after its installation. From this and other contemporary accounts it is clear that it was a Newcomen engine, constructed by Joseph Hornblower at Bearshood (Bearwood?) Hill, near Birmingham. Its cylinder was 48in diameter, and it was able to raise 3,000 hogsheads of water per hour.[22] The initial cost was £2,000 and the cost of coal came to £300 per year.

When Reinhold Angerstein visited the works in 1754, he was very impressed with the 'fire' engine he saw there, and made a special note of it when recording a list of the installations.[23] These included: '15 copper furnaces; 12 brass furnaces; 4 spelter or zinc furnaces; a bater [battery] mill, or small mill for kettles; rolling mills for making plates; rolling and cutting mills for wire, and a wire mill both of thick and fine drawn kinds'. The copper furnaces he saw were similar to those in use at Crew's Hole, and were employed in some twenty separate operations to produce metal of the quality required. Small quantities of ore were obtained from New Jersey whenever available, as these were of a higher copper content than the usual supplies shipped from Cornwall. A comparison of Cornish ore purchases suggests that during these early years of the company, the Warmley output was about one-quarter of the copper refined by the Bristol brass company.[24] This copper production appears to have remained fairly constant during this period, but there was further expansion elsewhere in the works. In the development of processes requiring rotative power there were additional signs that every means was being employed to conserve the meagre water supply, including the use of two horsemills as well as a windmill.

There has been much speculation over the years about the purpose of the tower, still to be seen in the vicinity. In 1881, the local historian Ellacombe wrote that there had been a windmill used for crushing ores at the Warmley works, but his account had scarcely been credited.[25] Viewed in the light of the company's inventory of 1761, however, Ellacombe's description fits perfectly. The premises then listed, included:

25 Houses and tenements;
One large Spelter work with 5 furnaces, arches warehouses,
2 Horse Mills, Loft for do; Caves &c.
22 Copper furnaces with Warehouses &c for them;
15 Brass furnaces with Mills Lofts Warehouses for them
One large Wire Mill with 9 benches & 5 blocks capable of making 100 rings of
    wire weekly
3 Large wheels or Rowling Mills with Rowles from 2 foot to 4 foot
5 Water Battery Mills with 12 Hammers that will make 60 ton of Brass Battery
    yearly.
One fire engine of 48 inches cylinder
One windmill with Stamps &c with all the Smith Shops, buildings & houses.
Warehouses Yards Thorows [mill races] Lofts Ponds Walls Tools Materials
    Implements &c on ye premises.[26]

With works of such comprehensive character a large labour force must have been employed and it is, therefore, hardly surprising to see that twenty-five houses and tenements are listed in the company property. Probably they included The Row; cottages near the tower which were demolished in 1966. The building which survives to this day, the large central 'House for shops with tower and clock', as Ellacombe describes it was not recorded on the 1761 inventory and must have been built at a later date.

Ellacombe continues by relating the traditional legends which grew around the Dutch families who were said to have lived in the area.[27] These stories revolve around the belief that John Champion, dressed in ragged clothes and playing the part of a beggar, visited Holland to discover the secrets of spelter and brassmaking, and persuaded Dutch workers to come back with him. Here the brothers John and William were being confused as they were on many occasions, but it is well known that William Champion travelled to the continent. The remainder of the story appears to be a mixture of fact and fantasy similar to those tales which surround other early industrialists who made visits to Europe. It was said, too, that Warmley Tower was known locally as the 'Tower of Babel', from the continual hubbub of foreign voices heard there. Perhaps this story originated from Champion's original premises at Baber's Tower in Bristol.

The property listed in the inventory suggests that the rate of expansion at Warmley must have required large amounts of capital. The only four partners to which reference has been found in these earlier years are Sampson Lloyd from the Birmingham Quaker ironfounders, married to William's sister, Rachel; Thomas Goldney, Quaker and Bristol banker, partner in the Coalbrookdale iron works and related to the Champions by the second marriage of William's father to Martha Vandewall, née Goldney; Thomas Crosby, Quaker, married to Rachel, daughter of John Reeve and widow of Charles Harford; William Champion himself, who apparently provided the largest share of the capital.[28] Nehemiah Champion, his father, was probably one of the partners at the outset of the company but he died in 1747 before the works commenced production.

William's eldest brother, John, does not appear to have ever been directly connected with the company. John inherited his father's shares in the Bristol brass company, although he did not actively take part in its organisation but, instead, devoted himself to his own works in Holywell, North Wales, where he was also concerned in several mining projects.[29] He patented a process in 1739 for producing various non-ferrous alloys and later, in 1758, enrolled Patent No 726 for producing brass and zinc from an ore other than calamine. This was blende, or black jack, the zinc sulphide which until this time had been cast aside as waste, and was readily available in the mining areas of North Wales. Thus John was able to exploit his new patent at Holywell. Relationships between the two brothers appear to have been amicable, and John was said to have acted as an agent for the Warmley company.[30]

### THE WARMLEY COMPANY, 1761

By 1761, William was seeking new partners in order to attract additional capital. He declared that the equipment at Warmley was not employed to its full capacity, and to obtain the further supplies of copper he needed, suggested that eighty new copper furnaces should be built at Kingswood nearby. To supply these with fuel, he planned to interest three local landowners, the 'Lords of the Collieries', to take on partnerships, for then they could be persuaded to sell 'Good Coal, 20% cheaper than [to] any other works of like nature'.[31] Prepounding all the advantages of the site at Warmley, and for the first time using the title of the Warmley Company,[32] Champion wrote to Charles Whittuck of Hanham Hall, large landowner in the mining area near the Bristol company's Crew's Hole copper works; Charles Bragge of Cleve Hill, later Lord Bathurst, another coal owner; and Norbonne Berkeley, influential man of society, Member of Parliament for Gloucestershire, owner of the Berkeley liberties in the northern part of Kingswood coalfield who was later to become Lord Botetourt. Champion emphasised that their total production of coal should be reserved for the Warmley works to deprive the old brass company, which then 'would not have the power to hurt and distress their neighbours at Warmley'.[33] Relations between the two businesses were very strained, as letters passing between them indicate.

When writing to his uncle Richard Champion, a leading partner of the Bristol brass company, William complained that he had been needlessly deprived of coal when the older company bought supplies from the Warmley area. In addition, his men had been bribed to reveal secrets of his spelter process which had then been used by the brass company. They had also introduced an unfair discount which made it difficult for Warmley to sell at a profit.[34] Joseph Loscombe, former clerk, but later a partner and one of the leaders of the Bristol company, replied on behalf of Richard Champion, denying all the charges. He made his own complaints against the actions of William Champion who, he alleged, had enticed employees away to Warmley by offering higher wages.[35] There were probably faults on both sides and there are indications that William was difficult to get on with. Joseph Hornblower, maker of the Warmley engine, wrote, 'As to Mr Champion, I think there are few mortals queerer, I hope I shall have done with them soon'.[36]

William Champion may have been difficult, but the Bristol company was disliked by the Kingswood coal-mine owners. Charles Bragge wrote, 'our grand oppressors the Brass Wire Company who have for a long time past layed us off and bamboozled us all by turns'.[37] Charles Whittuck had similar feeling against the treatment he had received from the old Bristol company, and thus it is not surprising that William Champion gained the support he requested from the local 'Lords of the Collieries'. In June 1761, the coal owners held a meeting with the Bristol company where they deliberately demanded much higher prices for coal delivered to Crew's Hole and Baptist Mills.[38] These prices caused consternation to members of the older company, and as Charles Whittuck had obviously anticipated, they were eventually refused. The way was open for trade with Warmley.

The following month, Champion and Charles Whittuck met at Kingswood to decide on the site of new copper furnaces, choosing ground 'Near the sign of the Horseshoe'. Two weeks later, Whittuck wrote, 'Saturday last I dined with Mr Champion . . . the Foundation for the cupolas is dug out and next Monday the Mason will begin Walling; He is to build the wall and the 17 furnaces for £15 each furnace, which is £255, we are to bring the Stones and the Lime in place'.[39]

With the construction of these furnaces, plans for the new partnership were well under way. A capital of £100,000 was proposed, 800 shares at £125 each.[40] The Warmley works would gain new funds for further expansion, and extra supplies of raw materials from the new cupolas. The coal lords of the partnership would have extra outlets to sell their coal without the oppression of the old company.

Before the end of the year, however, problems not previously envisaged arose in the coal situation, created by the adventurers. These were the small lease-holders running collieries on the lands of the coal lords, and they were in danger of producing more than enough coal to supply the 1,800 to 2,000 carts of coal per week which could be taken by the seventeen new furnaces at Kingswood. By obtaining good prices from Warmley in advance, some colliery owners had been encouraged to install horse whims and windmills, which enabled them to increase production. A few small owners in the area were even planning to erect steam engines and other drainage devices, which would make additional improvements in output. Charles Whittuck warned that surplus stocks would have to be disposed of to the Bristol company in spite of all their plans.[41] Problems such as these were to multiply in the next few years, and to take on a more serious aspect as development got right out of hand.

An indication of the financial situation is next available some four years later in 1765.[42] By this time the company was greatly enlarged, and was starting to run into monetary difficulties. The original partners were still represented in the company, and Champion himself still held the controlling shares. Sampson Lloyd and Thomas Goldney were, by now, minor partners, and Crosby's shares were in the hands of executors. Taking up the lead in the enterprise behind William Champion were Lord Botetourt (formerly Norbonne Berkeley), Charles Bragge, and Samuel and Charles Whittuck. In addition, Charles Arthur, Lord Botetourt's superintendent of coal works, was listed, together with Michael Newton, local landowner, James Mathews and Silas Blandford. At this stage, some of the new partners had not subscribed all their promised capital, and some maiden shares had not been taken; a total of only £29,000 had been paid in compared with the £50,000 expected.

Page 87 *Kelston annealing furnaces:* (right) *the front arch which held the furnace door;* (below) *the rear arch where the fires were tended*

Page 88 *Saltford annealing furnaces: (left) from outside the mill; (below) from inside. Note the horizontal beam for opening the furnace door*

It had been necessary to borrow large sums at high interest in order to run the company and, by this time, it was considered that £200,000 was needed to carry on the works, allowing for further expansion. Such a sum could not be expected from existing members of the partnership, and to overcome the need for borrowing so heavily it was proposed to bring new capital by making the company shares transferable, on a similar basis to the old Bristol company.[43]

In this respect, however, the older company was in a special position. It had been in existence, with its partnership and funds organised in an approved fashion, before the Bubble Act of 1720. After this Act, partnerships required the authorisation of a charter of incorporation in order to make their shares transferable. The next step for the Warmley Company was to apply for a royal charter.[44]

### THE FINAL EXPANSION

Whilst arrangements were made to go ahead with the application for incorporation and the preparation of the necessary reports, William Champion continued with more practical matters, an occupation more in keeping with his character. He was granted a patent, No 867, in 1767, which referred to three quite separate technical processes. These included the use of wrought iron in the refining of copper in order to remove arsenic; the manufacture of brass wire utilising pit coal instead of charcoal, in some way that was unspecified; and the use of black jack, the zinc sulphide ore which John Champion had been concerned with some nine years previously.

Although no details have been discovered it seems very likely that new copper furnaces were constructed again in this period. Purchases of Cornish copper ores were greatly increased, bringing the estimated output of the company within comparison of that of some of the largest smelting concerns (Appendix One, pages 222–3).

With the additional production of copper, came an entirely new

F

venture for the brass industry of Bristol. The city had long been
a centre for pinmaking on a small scale and this had been established later at Gloucester and the surrounding area. This industry
used brass wire manufactured by the old Bristol company but, by
1767, pinmaking was being undertaken within the Warmley Company.[45] A contemporary observer described the process he saw in
operation at the large 'manufactory' on the site. Possibly this was
the clock-tower building which still stands, if the bell dated 1764
in the tower can be taken as evidence of time of construction. The
description was as follows:

> After the ore is several times melted, it is poured into a flat mould of stone, by
> which means it is formed into thin plates about four feet long, and three broad.
> These plates are cut lengthways into seventeen stripes, and these again, by par-
> ticular machines into many more very narrow ones, and drawn out into the
> length of seventeen feet, which are again drawn into wires, and done up in
> bundles of forty shillings value each. About an hundred of these bundles of wire
> are made here every week, and each of these bundles makes an hundred thousand
> pins. The wires are cut into proper lengths, and the whole process completed
> here, employing a great number of girls, who, with little machines worked by
> their feet, point and head the pins with such expedition that each of them will
> do a pound and a half in a day. The heads are spun by a woman, with a wheel
> resembling a common spinning wheel; and then separated from one another by
> a man, with another little machine like a pair of shears.[46]

During 1767, William Champion compiled a 'State of Warmley
Co's Stock, Debts & Effects'. The buildings, mills, fire engines,
working houses, windmill, water works, warehouses, and dwelling
houses 'for the Mechanics Families &c', were valued at about
£105,000. Sales stock on hand included copper ore; copper; manufactured copper such as Guinea manillas and Guinea rods; brass,
and brass manufactured into kettles, pans, Guinea kettles, Guinea
neptunes, lattin, wire; ingots; furnaces, stills, brewing utensils and
pins; together with spelter; the total amounting to £94,000. The
Guinea supplies confirm references in other sources that Champion
was supplying wares for African barter in the outward journey of
the Bristol slave trade.

The company's stocks of coal, charcoal, calamine, iron, lead,

steel, timber, etc, amounted to £8,000, and the total capital employed was estimated at £300,000, with debts outstanding for goods
supplied for about £93,000. Members of the Warmley Company
had advanced £100,000, and £200,000 had been borrowed or
taken up at interest.[47]

With the large amount of machinery involved in producing the
company's output, it is hardly surprising to find that extra provision
had been made to ensure adequate rotative power. In June 1767,
Sir Joseph Banks saw two powerful engines at Warmley, which
were said to be two of the largest in the country. One engine with
a cylinder of 74in diameter usually worked at 9, but sometimes 10
or 11 strokes a minute, raising 17 hogsheads of water back to the
reservoir with each stroke, by means of four 30in pumps. Another
engine with a 60in cylinder was out of order on Sir Joseph's visit.[48]

These were not the only steam engines working in the area
during the 1760s. Donn's map of the environs of Bristol showing
several engine houses at nearby collieries, suggests that the plans
of some of the coal adventurers had materialised by this time. No
doubt they had been encouraged by the steady trade in supplying
coal to the copper furnaces of the Warmley Company.[49]

When the first new furnaces were built at Kingswood in 1761,
Champion's original principle of encompassing the whole complex
at Warmley was partly abandoned. Although these Kingswood
furnaces were only about a mile away, new premises were later
taken at greater distances. These included the battery mills established in the village of Bitton, on the River Boyd, about two miles
away, and at Kelston, on the banks of the Avon, at a distance of
about five miles. A brass foundry belonging to the company was
sited at St Augustine's Back, right in the centre of Bristol.

These new enterprises assisted Champion in his claim made in
application for the royal charter, that his works provided an occupation for some 2,000 poor men, women and children.[50] In this
number he must have included mining workers and outworkers, in
an effort to inflate the figure in a similar way to the Bristol brass

company's early petitions for protective import duties (pages 41 and 46).

DISASTER

In April 1767, a warrant was issued which gave authority for the preparation of the Charter of Incorporation. This took the plans of the company a stage further by allowing it to seek Parliamentary approval for raising a stock of transferable shares, and for the charter to be issued. Until this time, negotiations had been protracted but secrecy had been deliberately maintained. 'The less this is talked of the better', wrote Charles Bragge to Lord Botetourt, when informing him of arrangements.[51]

Once the warrant became common knowledge, petitions began to appear from all quarters of the industry, including the two local concerns, the Bristol brass company and the Freeman copper company. Champion's opponents argued that the proposed new capital of £400,000 for Warmley would cause damage to other similar concerns, as the trade had reached its full growth and no further development could be expected. Members of the Bristol brass company had reason to be worried, as the capital planned was double that of their own concern, then considered to be the largest of its kind. They referred to their own petition for a similar charter which had been applied for, some four years earlier, but had not met with any success. Nearly all the large companies were in opposition because they were convinced that Warmley would deprive them of their trade.

After lengthy legal proceedings the attorney general concluded that there was no objection in point of law to granting the letters patent requested by the Warmley Company. Thus a second warrant was issued for the preparation of the charter, in October 1767.

The opposition renewed its efforts even more vigorously, petitioning the Lords Committee of the Privy Seal and presenting new arguments against the granting of the charter. If Warmley was successful, they claimed, the company would develop into a monopoly, because of its enormous size. Alternatively, it was likely to disintegrate into a financial bubble. The heavy debts incurred by the company were cited against it, and it was disputed that there was any reason for granting such privileges in preference to other existing partnerships, when Warmley had not ventured into any new or specially hazardous branch of commerce.[52] By March 1768, the opposition had won its case; no further proceedings could be taken to obtain a Charter of Incorporation.

The following month, Champion was dismissed from the services of the company by his partners who discovered that he had tried to withdraw part of his capital without permission, knowing that collapse was inevitable.[53]

In July, there were desperate attempts on the part of Charles Bragge to save the company from absolute ruin. He wrote to Lord Botetourt forwarding a scheme to reform the partnership on a more moderate scale, having himself been 'completely ruined by the consequence of my former infatuation'. He hoped that it would be possible for the partners to regain at least part of their losses by continuing to run the works at Warmley. Lord Botetourt, however, was in no position to subscribe new capital, and was shortly to flee to America to escape his debts,[54] neither could support be obtained from the remaining partners. In March of 1769, following the bankruptcy of William Champion, the works of the Warmley Company were offered for sale by auction.

Thus, the era had come to an end when the Warmley copper and brass works could be regarded as the 'most complete of any in this kingdom',[55] or as the showplace, visited by a series of travellers who had left descriptions throughout the development of the site. Almost ten years afterwards, at least one partner, Sampson Lloyd, was still making a valiant attempt to see that his finances in Bristol were settled in a satisfactory way.[56] By this time Warmley had been purchased by the old Bristol brass company, but was never again used so extensively as in the day of William Champion.

## To be Sold by Auction,

### At the *EXCHANGE* COFFEE-HOUSE,

On MONDAY the 24th of April next,

## The WARMLY COMPANY's
## COPPER and BRASS WORKS,

*Well known to be the moſt compleat of any in
this Kingdom.*

THE Furnaces for ſmelting Copper are ſituated near the
Center of *Kingſwood*, which is full of Coal, and
which can be delivered at theſe Furnaces, and at *Warmly*
Braſs Works, at Four Shillings per Ton, which is cheaper
than any Works in the Neighbourhood can be ſupplied, or
even thoſe in *Wales*, who give at leaſt Five Shillings and Six-
pence for Coal not near ſo durable as the *Kingſwood* Coal.——
The Braſs Manufaĉtory and Copper Forges are ſituated at
*Warmly* and *Bitton*, in the County of *Gloceſter*, and *Kelſon*,
in the County of *Somerſet*, and lie at no great Diſtance one
from another. They conſiſt of Two Copper Forges, and Seventeen Mill Wheels for Braſs, Battery, Wire, Copper, and
Braſs Rolls; together with a large Pin Manufaĉtory, and
five Spelter Furnaces, with neceſſary Tools in all the different Branches in perfeĉt good Order.———There are good
Workmen in all the Branches at preſent on the Spot. The
Warehouſes in *London*, *Dublin*, *Briſtol*, and *Liverpool*, are
ſo well eſtabliſhed, that the Demand for Goods made at the
above Works is more than they have been able to ſupply.——
There are Seventy-nine Acres of Freehold Lands at *Warmly*,
all lying together, on Part of which the Works there ſtand;
beſides ſeveral Parcels of Leaſehold Lands, ſome for Terms
of Years, and ſome for Lives, upon which the Copper Furnaces and the Mills at *Bitton* and *Kelſon* are built; together
with a large Houſe at *Warmly* for a Manager, and convenient
Houſes for the Workmen at each of the ſaid Places.

Any Perſon willing to treat for or examine the ſeveral Pre-
miſes, may apply to the Committee of the ſaid Company, who
meet every Monday at Eleven o'Clock in the Forenoon, and
ſit till Two, at the *Warmly* Warehouſe on St. *Auguſtine's-
Back*, *Briſtol*; or any other Day at the ſame Place, to Mr.
Matthews, who will take Care to have the Works ſhewn
them.

☞ If theſe Works ſhould be ſold by private Contraĉt before the Day of Sale above-mentioned, public Notice ſhall be
given of ſuch Contraĉt being entered into.

N. B. It is to be obſerved, that the above Four Shillings
per Ton for Coal, is calculated at the Rate of Five-pence
Half-penny per Horſeload, which is Three Buſhels; and who
ever purchaſes the ſaid Works, may be aſſured of being ſerv-
ed at Four Shillings per Ton, or at Five-pence Half-penny
per Horſeload.

*Auction sale notice from Felix Farley's* Bristol Journal

# CHAPTER FIVE

# The Decline of the Old Bristol Company

'What Manchester is in cotton, Bradford in wool and Sheffield in Steel, Birmingham is in brass.'

W. C. Aitken, *Brass and Brass Manufactures* (1866)

THERE were ten different organisations in opposition to the granting of the charter to Warmley. They varied from the large copper mining and smelting concerns to the common council of Gloucester which petitioned in support of the pin manufacturers of its city. Of these ten petitioners, four described themselves specifically as brass producers and manufacturers.

## The Brass Manufacturers' Combination

The four manufacturers were led by the Bristol company, The Brass Battery, Wire & Copper Company of Bristol, to quote its full title used in the 1760s. The other three businesses were John Freeman & Copper Company of Bristol; Thomas Patten & Company of Warrington; and Charles Roe & Copper Company of Macclesfield. There were other brass manufacturers in various parts of the country not represented in the petitions, but they were local concerns involved in a smaller type of business.

The Bristol brass company summarised its early contribution to the development of the industry in the case put before the Crown opposing the Warmley charter.[1] By the 1760s, the company had achieved the position where the value of its stock was said to amount to £200,000, with transferable shares representing one eight-hundredth part changing hands for £250, and it was dividing a profit of £8,000 annually.[2] Thus it would appear that the Bristol business was by far the largest of its kind, apart from the Warmley Company,[3] but two other companies, Thomas Patten's and Charles Roe's, were developing rapidly at the time.

The John Freeman & Copper Company was still primarily concerned with the copper trade only. This business was the successor to the old company founded by the Costers. The new name was adopted in 1764 from the leading partner after the death of Joseph Percival, just as Percival had succeeded members of the Coster family. After John Freeman assumed control, the company decided to enter the field of brass production, to absorb surplus stocks of copper which were expected to accrue. This was a form of self-protection against the rapid growth of new manufacturers appearing in the copper trade, especially the Warmley Company, expanding so quickly on local territory.[4] Plans were made to manufacture the new product at White Rock at the Swansea smelting site of the company but, nevertheless, the making of brass always remained a very small part of this business.

The other two petitioners were in a different category. With the Bristol brass company they formed the group of manufacturers responsible for the greatest part of brass production in the country. They were so described by Dr Watson, when he stated that they were the only companies 'which go through all the processes of smelting the copper from its ore, of preparing the calamine, and of uniting it with copper for the making of brass'.[5]

The older of the two other companies possessed foundations going back to 1719 in a copper-smelting business established at Warrington under the leadership of Thomas Patten. Patten and some of his partners were later concerned in a separate, but closely associated company set up at Cheadle in North Staffordshire for the production and manufacture of brass. Other closely connected works were started in that area, their formation being stimulated by copper ore and calamine to be found in the southern tip of the Pennines, with coal available locally.[6]

In 1765, William Champion wrote to Patten in an attempt to dissuade him from setting up four new copper and brass-battery mills on the Holywell site which had formerly been used by Champion's elder brother, John. William suggested to Thomas Patten that the industry was already over-productive, the reason why his brother had already withdrawn from the works. The true motive for this advice, however, can be gauged from proposals put to Patten that he could alternatively invest his money in the Warmley Company.[7] His advice was not heeded, for Patten continued with his plans. Eventually, when his separate concerns were amalgamated into one company in 1780, it was launched with a capital of £40,000, large for its time, but not approaching that of the brass company at Bristol.[8] From the early 1770s and, possibly, prior to that time, the Cheadle company is believed to have been trading in collaboration with the Bristol company, in a combination of brass manufacturers which imposed its prices on the market, co-ordinating its activities with those of the long-established copper smelters' association.

By the end of the 1770s, the other principal brass producer, the Macclesfield Copper Company, had also joined this combination. Its partners had dispatched a deputation for this purpose to the committee of the 'Bristol Brass Wire Coy' on 3 April 1778. By 8 April, the committee of the Macclesfield company was ordering that their 'middling wire' should be offered to their customers at Birmingham, Wolverhampton and Walsall at the same price as the Bristol company.[9]

The Macclesfield Copper Company had been formed in 1758, by Charles Roe and his partners. Initially, the business had depended on supplies of copper ore from Alderley Edge and, later, obtained additional stocks from the Coniston mines in the Lake District. By 1762, Roe had extended the activities of his concern to include the manufacture of brass wire, and the rolling of copper and brass which was carried out at Eaton, near Congleton, 5 miles from Macclesfield. Calamine was being obtained from deposits near

Mold in Flintshire, and from Moelydd and Llanymynech in Shropshire. There were further extensions to company premises in 1766, at Bosley, 6 miles south of Macclesfield, where brass-rolling and battery mills were erected. The following year, in evidence for the petition opposing the Warmley charter, the company revealed that it had already expended a sum of £15,500 in building up their concern, and expected to make considerable additions to that amount before the works were completed.[10] The business was thriving, but by no means comparable, as yet, with the old Bristol company. Within its organisation, however, events had already taken place which set in train a series of developments which were eventually to destroy the supremacy of the Bristol business.

### Parys Mountain Mining

In October 1763, Charles Roe and one of his partners had visited Mynydd Trysglwyn—more popularly known as Parys Mountain—at Amlwch on the north coast of Anglesey, and which had long been thought to contain deposits of copper ore. Sir Nicholas Bayly, owner of the eastern part of the hill, and part-owner of the western half, had already lost money in trying to find workable sources of the ore, and agreed that the eastern territory he owned should be leased to Charles Roe and his company in return for one-eighth of any ore produced. Operations commenced the following year, and by 1767 there were signs that some success had been achieved, and that more was anticipated by the company. Accounts relate a dramatic discovery on 2 March 1768, when an extensive body of ore was found a few feet below the surface.

Although the metal content of this ore was later shown to be very much lower than that of the Cornish deposits, by comparison it was easily worked, and available in such large quantities that the find constituted a major discovery which was to have far-reaching consequences.

The Macclesfield business proceeded to organise its works to take advantage of these new opportunities, but the success of its mining exploits brought a series of disputes with the landowner, Sir Nicholas Bayly. In addition to his agreed one-eighth share of ore to be taken as his dues, he demanded to be admitted to a share of the Macclesfield company. Protracted negotiations ensued, but the differences were not resolved and, on finding himself excluded from the copper-smelting company, Bayly started to mine the other territory of the hill. Immediately, he involved himself in legal difficulties with the owners of the property where he was merely a lessee with no claim to mineral rights. The litigation was to last for the next seven years, and his adversaries introduced a solicitor to defend their interests who was completely inexperienced in any kind of industrial management, Thomas Williams of Llanidan, Anglesey. By the end of 1778 he was active partner of the mining company, managing the mine on behalf of his clients. The share of land belonging to Sir Nicholas Bayly was also leased to his business. The Parys Mine Company had been formed outside the old combination.[11]

The Macclesfield Company, meanwhile, had continued to mine the eastern property which it had leased from Sir Nicholas Bayly. The company works near Macclesfield were relegated to brass production and the manufacture of brass and copperwares, whilst new copper-smelting premises were established at Liverpool. This branch of the business came under the direction of William Roe, the eldest son of Charles Roe.

In the early years at Parys Mountain, the ore was calcined in large open kilns. This had the two-fold effect of concentrating the mass before transporting it by sea to Liverpool, and by eliminating part of the sulphur content, enabled the subsequent smelting processes to be carried out more efficiently. The kilns were situated on the hill above the mine, with the result that the large amounts of sulphur dioxide released into the atmosphere quickly destroyed the vegetation in the surrounding hundreds of acres.[12] It was in connection with an improvement to this process that John Champion,

junior, negotiated with all the owners interested in the Anglesey mining complex.[13] Although relevent to the history of the Bristol industry in view of the possibility that it may have resulted from collaboration between the Bristol Champion family, this new process was, of course, of minor importance to the great new industry being created in Anglesey. The vast quantity of copper ore so easily obtained, was bringing great wealth to the companies concerned. By 1782, the Macclesfield Company was dividing net profits of £15,000 per annum.[14]

The Warrington Company under Thomas Patten had established new works at Stanley near St Helens for smelting its copper ore. This site was mainly responsible for processing the one-eighth share of ores from the Macclesfield Company mines which was due to Sir Nicholas Bayley.

Thomas Williams and the Parys Mine Company had opened smelting works at Ravenhead in Lancashire by 1780, which was managed by Joseph Harris, a staunch Baptist from Kingswood, Bristol. The company had also taken over the Upper Bank smelting Works at Swansea, and built new plant for the manufacture of copperware on the Holywell stream in Flintshire, where earlier works had been situated. This company had expanded at an unprecedented rate under the leadership of Thomas Williams. He was soon to take control of the copper industry on an even greater scale.[15]

### Growth of the Birmingham Industry

The great expansion of these northern industries disturbed the established organisation of the copper smelters' association, particularly as Thomas Williams refused to co-operate with its members. The interests of his company, which mined its own supply of ore, were quite different to those of most of the members of the association. The Bristol brass company had long withdrawn from ownership of Devon and Cornish mines and, in common with most other smelting businesses, purchased its requirements of ore. Williams refused to come to terms with the members unless they purchased his Anglesey ores at a price which he thought reasonable. While the smelters were taking this blow to their normal business methods, the combination of brass manufacturers came under attack at Birmingham.[16]

From the seventeenth century, the West Midlands had been a centre for a gradually increasing variety of skilled metal-working trades. In the early eighteenth century, these manufactures were greatly extended, and Birmingham began to export brassware to the continent. Daniel Defoe wrote in 1728, 'We daily send great quantities of wrought iron and brass to Holland, France, Italy, Venice and to all parts of Germany', and he thought it unnecessary to emphasise the importance of the Birmingham wrought-iron and brass manufactures. Much of the early brass used in the Midlands would have been imported from the Low Countries, but from the early eighteenth century an increasing proportion of these supplies would have been brought from Bristol. At this period, the Birmingham area had no local industry producing the metal.[17]

A works for producing brass metal was, however, established on a modest scale in Coleshill Street, Birmingham, about 1740, by the Turner family. In April 1754, Reinhold Angerstein visited the premises where he found three brass houses, each containing three coal-fired furnaces, using copper ore from Wales and calamine from Derbyshire.[18] The Turners were said to produce 300 tons of brass per annum, but the Midland's requirements for the more expensive grades suitable for cold working continued to be satisfied mainly from Bristol and Cheadle.[19] Later when the Macclesfield Company had established its production of brass, it also obtained a share of the market. By the 1780s, Dr Watson related that

Great quantities of good brass are made by most nations in Europe, as well as by the English; but the English brass is more adapted to the Birmingham manufacturies, than any other sort is . . . The manner of mixing different sorts of brass, so as to make the mixture fit for particular manufactures is not known to foreigners; though this is a circumstance of great importance.[20]

This dependence, during most of the eighteenth century, on brass produced outside the West Midlands was, to a large extent based on geographical factors. There were no easy transport routes to bring copper ore and calamine from distant sources to Birmingham. Streams and rivers suitable for water power were also limited, so that the basic processes of manufacture, rolling, battery and wiredrawing, tended to be carried out at the centres which produced the metals.[21]

### ACTION AGAINST THE COMBINATION

The Midlands manufacturers produced an increasing variety of stamped goods and such wares as door and window furniture, locks, bolts and hinges, and heavy foundry goods, in addition to the traditional 'toys' of the Birmingham area.[22] One writer estimated that, by 1780, the consumption of brass in Birmingham was in the region of 1,000 tons per annum.[23] In the ten years prior to that date, increasing difficulties had been experienced in the Cornish copper industry as the greater depth of mines brought additional problems. Production of ore in Cornwall had fallen and the standard price had increased, which in turn had affected the cost of producing brass for those companies which mainly relied on Cornish supplies. In 1780, the combination of brass manufacturers increased its prices to the Birmingham market by £12, to £84 per ton. This move was possibly instigated by the Bristol company, the brass-making business most affected by the situation in the Cornish mines.

Manufacturers in the Birmingham trade were highly indignant at these measures, the general feeling being that the very high increase in ingot-brass was not fully justified by the advances in copper. Representatives of nineteen businesses held a meeting at 'The Swan' in Bull Street on 18 August 1780, in protest against the necessity of raising their own prices to cover the costs of their raw materials.[24] The meeting was followed by a public attack on the manufacturers' combination, in the form of a lengthy advertisement in *Aris's Gazette*, 9 October 1780. In this a tirade on the increase in prices was followed by a wordy protest against the harsh treatment meted out by the combination of manufacturers in the Birmingham area. The writer alleged that, in the past, the combination had both raised and lowered its prices just when it suited it, at one period lowering them to such an extent that the local Turners' brass manufactory would have been forced out of business had it not been for the protection of certain Birmingham warehouses. Again, when a new company at Birmingham had erected works for making brass, the price of brass had been reduced by the combination on three different occasions by £15 per ton. 'In former years the Company, (now called the O.C.) assumed the Whole controlling Power, they rose and fell Prices at Discretion. . . . Some boldly stood forth the Champions of Liberty, and in Defiance of Oppression ventured to erect Works and risque their Fortunes therein.'

It has been suggested that the reference to 'Champions of Liberty' may have been alluding to the Champions of Warmley and their business, which had broken away from the old Bristol company.[25] The attack of the advertisement appears to have been mainly directed against the Bristol concern, the 'O.C.', or old company, although this term was sometimes used collectively, both for the combination of brass manufacturers, and the copper smelters' association.

Referring to the activities of the combination, the writer continued: 'The O.C. tell you that "If you dare to sell at less Price than they have fixed you shall not be served at all".' Then came the call to freedom,

I appeal to your feelings as Men, to your Consequence as Tradesmen . . . shall so respectable a Body of Merchants and manufacturers become the Dupes of a Set of capricious Monopolists in the Articles of Brass and Spelter on which their Trade depends? No! you must rouse yourselves. . . . Be no longer governed by Strangers when you have the Power to help yourselves at Home . . . the making of Copper and Brass is familiar and without risque, what then should prevent the Merchants and manufacturers from making their own Metals.[26]

A plan was put forward the following month at 'a meeting of merchants and manufacturers concerned in the consumption of metals in Birmingham and places adjacent'.[27] It was suggested by one Peter Capper that each manufacturer concerned should subscribe a minimum of £100 to form a company for making brass. In fact, Capper was the 'Friend of the Trade', the writer of the 'Serious Address' in the newspaper advertisement, although he kept this secret prior to the meeting. He was a merchant dealing in metals and residing at Redland in Bristol, having moved from the Birmingham area.[28]

At the meeting, a committee was appointed to formulate a basis for the company proposed. In the meantime, Peter Capper had already written to Matthew Boulton, urging his support for the formation of this new Midlands industry 'that they may no longer be under ye arbitrary hand of the Bristoll company'.[29] Boulton held back initially, being mainly preoccupied with his difficulties in supplying engines to the Cornish mines, and the latter's problems with Anglesey competition. However, Boulton was a large consumer of brass, particularly with his manufacture of buttons and, subsequently, when asked to take a lead, he was drawn into the new organisation.[30]

In the three months that followed the launching of the proposals, a steady stream of correspondence passed between Capper and Boulton. Boulton made frequent inquiries on various aspects of organisation within the brassmaking industry. Capper supplied 'intelligence' on manufacturing methods and sources of supply which he gained from the Bristol company with help from his friend and associate, George Watson of Bristol.[31] This information mainly consisted of small details, lacking the technical expertise of the descriptions compiled by the Swedish investigators. Boulton, however, presumably found the source of information worthwhile, and Capper was careful to acknowledge the presents which were received by various members of his family.

On 24 December 1780, for instance, Capper was keeping Boulton informed about conversation passing between members of the OC on the danger of the new Birmingham company. In reply to a query, he was able to report that supplies of calamine were plentiful, and there was no likely danger of the Bristol company capturing the whole market. In early January he was writing 'I see no probability for Mr Watson to get a sight of ye O.C. Articles, they have been made I should suppose, 80 yrs back, and therefore impossible to come at, or a Copy'. Later in January, Capper was referring to details of the manufacture of zinc, which he had already passed on, and of brass production wrote 'I wish I was able to give you ye expense of a tun, but I cannot, being unable to come at ye quantity of Coal that would be expended'.[32]

George Watson wrote in March, giving details of the route and transport costs of a large quantity of calamine from the Powis mines near Llanymynech, which had just been landed in Bristol, having been sent by trow from Shrewsbury. The old company had used this source for about two years and 300 to 400 tons were expected. The price of ore was not known by his informant but transport costs amounted to about £1 per ton. Watson had taken the opportunity to procure a basketful to send on by trow to Boulton.[33] Later, Capper urged that a former clerk of the Bristol company, who had been 'their servant for 30 years and turned off without notice', should be given employment with the new company, despite a bond for £400 not to join any other brass business.[34] Boulton did not take the advice.

Above all, both Watson and Capper repeated frequently that the Birmingham industry should smelt its own copper, and that the most suitable site for the combined operations was at Swansea, in view of the favourable prices of coal there.[35] Boulton was in opposition to the new company entering the copper-smelting business, being already associated himself with the Fenton Copper Company, but he agreed with the assessment of Swansea for the site of the proposed works. Meanwhile, he was making investigations into the industry at other centres.

G

On 11 April 1781, the subscribers attended a meeting to sign the articles of partnership of the new Birmingham company. It was to be called the Birmingham Metal Company, and its members were described as 'Joint Traders in the Trade, Art and Mystery of making and selling Brass, Spelter and other Metals'. A capital of £20,000 was to be divided into 200 shares, with no one person owning more than 4, and with every holder agreeing to purchase one ton of brass in every year; the first company with this kind of co-operative basis. Encouraged by the new canals being built in the Midlands area providing a good transport system, the members decided that the works should be built in Birmingham. Boulton disagreed, and shortly afterward resigned from the committee. Peter Capper severed his connections for similar reasons, but the Birmingham Metal Company had established its organisation. Its very formation provided a blow to the brass company at Bristol, by immediately threatening an important market for its products.

Shortly afterwards, the Parys Mines Company made an offer to supply the new Birmingham company with copper, on more attractive terms than normally given to other concerns. Thus a connection was established between the two businesses remaining outside the combination and trade associations of the older companies. When the new works were completed at Birmingham, the brass combination reduced its price from £84 to £56 per ton, in an attempt to place the new company in difficulties. However, the Birmingham Metal Company already had an advantage in the price of copper it used. In addition, the shareholders were covenanted to purchase 200 tons of brass per annum, and the effects of the old methods of commercial pressure within the industry could be overcome more easily. The Cheadle and Bristol companies continued to supply part of the Birmingham market, as some of the traders in the town were not concerned with the new undertaking, but the old, almost complete, dependence on materials produced outside the area had been finally broken.[36]

*The Cornish Metal Company*

Under the leadership of Thomas Williams, the Parys Mines Company continued to take advantage of its low production costs to expand its market. From the early years of the century, the mine owners in Cornwall had blamed the copper manufacturers, particularly those in Bristol, for working together and refusing to pay a fair price for their ores. As the association of copper smelters made further attempts to keep ore costs down to compete against the Anglesey industry, the situation in the Cornish mines deteriorated rapidly, and the old antagonism increased.

Thomas Williams tried to persuade Boulton to use his wide influence with the mine owners and manufacturers to end the struggle between the two sides of the industry; assured prices would have suited his plans. When these efforts failed, Williams declared that 'No power on earth shall restrain us'. The Cornish mines were bound to be damaged in any continued price-cutting contest, as they needed to install and run expensive equipment for pumping water to keep their deep workings open. The mines in Anglesey, quite near to the surface, worked under no such disadvantage.[37]

By 1784, Williams had captured the market for copper sheathing for naval vessels, having obtained patent rights for producing rolled and drawn copper bolts which overcame problems in securing the metal. This advanced technique which he had acquired, subsequently gave him the opportunity to supply sheathing to the French, Dutch and Spanish navies in addition to those of his own country. During this period, Williams took over the management of the remainder of the Parys Mountain mining complex when, in 1784, the lease to the Macclesfield Company had run the full length of its term. He formed a partnership with the landowner, Lord Uxbridge, who had succeeded Sir Nicholas Bayly, and others, including the iron-founder John Wilkinson, to establish the Mona Mine Company which Williams then proceeded to organise along

the lines of the Parys Mines Company. Sites were taken over which
formerly belonged to the old Warrington company, the copper-
smelting business which had been associated with the brass-making
company at Cheadle. As the Anglesey companies continued expanding, many Cornish mines closed down.

In face of these serious difficulties, various plans were put forward by mine owners and manufacturers to assist the industry in
Cornwall. The outcome was a series of meetings held in Truro
during the summer of 1785, at which representatives of the smelting
and mining concerns consulted for the purpose of establishing the
Cornish Metal Company. Finally, an agreement was signed to take
effect from 1 September. The Cornish mine owners formed themselves into an association, agreeing to sell their ores only through
the Metal Company. In return the company undertook to buy all
ores offered to it, at prices which were to be agreed, and to take
responsibility for organising the smelting, refining, manufacturing
and marketing of all copper from the Cornish mines. To carry out
these obligations contracts were signed with five existing companies including both the Bristol businesses, the brass company and
the John Freeman Copper Company. They were offered a guaranteed rate for processing the ore plus an 8 per cent profit.

Agreement was also reached with the Anglesey industries 'to
equalise prices, limit output and establish an agreed pattern of
sales'. Joint warehouses for the sale of copper were to be set up
at London, Liverpool, Birmingham and Bristol, where all copper
produced by the Cornish Metal Company and the Anglesey concerns was to be sold at similar prices. The Cornish miners were
optimistic that the days of oppression and price reductions imposed
by the old smelters' association were at last at an end.[38]

From the earliest days there were signs that this plan would
not work successfully. Thomas Williams was immediately suspected
of continuing undercover negotiations to sell his copper at cut
prices. The organisation of the Metal Company was hampered by
the large stocks of ores it had on hand, and failed lamentably to

market its prepared copper against the superior selling methods of the Anglesey companies. Prices of finished copper were raised, annoying the Birmingham manufacturers who, from the start, had mistrusted the possible influence of the Bristol brass company. Soon the Birmingham industry was discussing plans to establish its own smelting organisation. A number of the Cornish mines broke their purchasing agreements, and even the directors of the Metal Company negotiated with smelters who were not among the contracted companies. Towards the end of 1787, there were 6,000 tons of copper unsold in the stock of the Cornish Metal Company, and new attempts were being made to form some new agreement between Anglesey and Cornish interests.[39]

While the organisation in Cornwall was showing these signs of disintegration, the Bristol brass company decided to withdraw from its contract for ore smelting, but by the terms of the agreement was obliged to give one year's notice of its intention.[40] Throughout this period the Bristol business must have been working under extreme difficulties, following the loss of its former influence over the whole of the industry.

## The Sale of the Bristol Company

There are few known sources of information on events and reactions in Bristol throughout this difficult period but, during 1786, shares of the brass company were offered for sale in the local newspaper.[41] At a general meeting of the joint proprietors held at the Queen Street Warehouse on 18 December 1786, all members present resolved 'That it appears impracticable for the said company to carry on their trade any longer and that the same should be dissolved and terminated'.[42]

The committee responsible for the management of the concern prior to this period consisted of nine members, five of them from the Harford family. They were led by Mark Harford, and at this time the company was often described as the Mark Harford &

Bristol Brass Company. He is believed to have been the grandson of the Mark Harford who became involved in the affairs of the brass company through his marriage to Love, grand-daughter of John Andrews, one of the Bristol company's founders. Other company involvement with the Harford banking family had been brought about by the marriage of Edward Harford to Elizabeth, grand-daughter of Edward Lloyd, another founder of the business. Edward's son and two grandsons were members of the company committee, and were joined by Joseph Harford from another branch of the family.

Early in 1787, advertisements appeared in the newspapers of many parts of the country for a sale to be held on 26 February, of all brass company property—'All the Works, Mills, Estates and Utensils of the United Brass Battery, Wire and Copper Company of Bristol'.[43] The sale was noted by the Macclesfield Company who planned to send a representative. A few days later, it was announced that the works had been sold for a mere £16,000.[44]

In fact the property passed, through a complicated sales procedure, to a group of Bristol merchants almost identical with the formation of the old company committee, consisting of ten members, six of them Harfords, and still led by Mark Harford. The other Harfords were Edward, Joseph, John Scandrett, Charles Edward, and Charles Joseph, new to the group. Other members were Abraham Ludlow, John Fisher Weare, William Battersby, and Thomas Walker. The new owners proceeded to organise their business under the name of Harfords & Bristol Brass & Copper Company, with Articles of Partnership dated 31 March 1788. Thus the new business forefeited the right of distributing transferable shares which had been held by the old company from the time of exemption granted them from the Bubble Act. The projected new capital of £100,000 was divided into a hundred shares, with seventy-five being taken up by the partners at the time.[45]

Meanwhile, in the Cornish Metal Company, Thomas Williams had been requested to assume responsibility for marketing the large stocks of copper held by the organisation. During the following four years, Williams controlled the industry in an almost complete monopoly, keeping down ore prices paid to the mine owners, whilst raising the cost of refined copper. To a large extent he achieved his purpose in selling the stocks of metal and bringing the Cornish mining industry to a more healthy position, but the rising prices which he created soon caused further unrest in Birmingham. In 1790, he also took over the purchase of ore from the Cornish mines, which until this time had remained in the hands of the Cornish Metal Company. New contracts were arranged for smelting, this time with ten copper companies, including Harfords & Bristol Brass & Copper Company and also the Freeman Copper Company.[46] It is from this time that the Harford company became concerned with Swansea premises. All the main businesses were smelting copper in this area of South Wales to take advantage of low prices in coal and the ease of access provided for shipping bringing ores into Swansea Bay. Harfords took over part of a site at Upper Forest, which had been developed for the purpose by the Morris-Lockwood smelting company and was no longer required by that business.[47] It seems likely that from this time the Harford company discontinued copper smelting in the Bristol area.

Peter Capper had informed Matthew Boulton that the old Bristol brass company had difficulties with carriage costs of coal to its old smelting works prior to the 1780s. By 1781 the company had transferred its smelting processes to the works at Warmley to be nearer coal resources, but this had been only a temporary measure.[48]

Some years before, Gabriel Jars had visited Bristol to report on metallurgical techniques in his official tour on behalf of the French government. He found that smelting was being carried out by very similar methods to those described previously by the Swedish travellers, but Jars also discovered that experiments were being conducted at Bristol in order to reduce the large number of furnace operations. It was hoped to develop techniques whereby refined copper could be obtained with only two roasting, and five melting operations, and two large furnaces for roasting had already been constructed.[49] Such a system could have saved a large amount of coal, and is basically similar to the Welsh Process of smelting, evolved at Swansea at a rather later date. Possibly the Bristol experiments contributed to the success of the Welsh Process.

Dissatisfaction with the smelting industries finally persuaded the Birmingham manufacturers to establish their own copper company, the Birmingham Mining & Copper Company, organised in a similar way to its forerunner, the Birmingham Metal Company, but with smelting premises in the Swansea area. The formation of this new company in 1790, gave an additional worthwhile market to the mine owners in Cornwall, outside the monopoly of Thomas Williams. Thus by the end of 1791, the availability of this market in addition to the improved outlook brought about by William's own efforts, meant that he was unable to gain support for his new project to completely control the industry. The Cornish Metal Company lost its cohesion, and the industry turned to an open market in a policy advocated from Birmingham.[50]

Copper prices still continued to rise in the years that followed and, in 1799, the government instituted an inquiry into the industry. The Midlands held Thomas Williams responsible for the difficulties, and his business methods were closely investigated. Williams himself was, by this time, a member of the House of Commons, and well able to deal with the investigations. The committee report proved inconclusive. However, while giving evidence on the history of the English industry, Williams referred to the early foundations of the old brass company at Bristol, and went on to describe it as 'now, perhaps the most considerable brass house in all Europe'.[51] But already it had started to decline.

The banking influence of the Harford family within the brass company's organisation came to the fore after the retirement of Mark Harford. From 1796, the company was often referred to as the Joseph Harford & Bristol Brass Company; the main concern of Joseph being his partnership in the bank of Ames, Cave & Company.[52] The remaining Harfords of the brass company, Edward Harford and his descendants, were all connected with the Harford Bank. From this time, the brass works appear to have been regarded purely as an investment. Few technical innovations were subsequently adopted.

The new century brought hard times in the trade generally, both in Bristol and at Cheadle,[53] but the Birmingham industry continued to prosper, increasing the market for its products particularly for cast wares which were so easily produced. There, new methods were adopted to manufacture a large range of domestic fittings such as those needed for the new gas-lighting, and the industrial components which were required in increasing variety with the expansion of rotative steampower. Meanwhile, the Harford & Bristol Brass Company retained its interest in traditional wares, producing wire and battery ware by the slow traditional methods. The company continued to decline in importance.

The need to consolidate the wide range of works belonging to the Harford company must have been frequently considered during this difficult period, although few negotiations have been discovered. It was said that the Warmley works was never used to its full advantage after the days of the Warmley Company. A large amount of cast-iron steam-engine fittings, including a cylinder 6ft 2½in by 10ft, was offered to Matthew Boulton for sale in 1784, by the old company, thus diminishing the available rotative power at Warmley. Prior to the turn of the century, part of the works were leased to a pin manufacturing business, the remainder being retained for the time being to continue the company's smelting of zinc.[54]

Land-tax records indicate that Crew's Hole and Conham smelting works were leased to another business from the early 1780s, but, by 1799, the Conham site was sold outright to a new chemical concern planning to produce 'artificial spermicetti'.[55] The Harford company continued to smelt copper for the time being at the Swansea smelting site. A reminder of this production can still be found in trade tokens which were issued by the company in 1811 inscribed, 'BB & Copper Co, payable at Bristol, Swansea and London'. By 1820, this work had ceased and the site was relinquished, bringing an end to the smelting of copper within the Bristol company.[56] In 1828, the derelict works at Crew's Hole were sold to a Dr Benjamin Somers for £1,880. In 1832, Warmley was sold to the leaseholders of the pin factory, who continued to smelt zinc on the site.[57]

Of the smaller mills, Woodborough battery mill, near Compton Dando on the River Chew, had been abandoned and was described as derelict by the early 1790s.[58] Land-tax returns of the battery mill at Weston, Bath, record a change of ownership about 1811 or 1812, and the Bitton battery mills changed hands in 1825 when they were taken over by papermakers who had been using a mill on the River Boyd further upstream from Bitton.[59]

The earliest site of the business established at Baptist Mills was said to have been abandoned by about 1814 when the work carried out there was transferred to the Keynsham premises. Ownership was retained by the company but, by 1830, Baptist Mills was derelict in part for a surveyor's report described the mills and buildings on the $13\frac{1}{2}$ acre site as 'not saleable as a manufactory'.[60] The following year part of the works with houses and land was advertised for sale,[61] but with little success apparently. A further advertisement four years later, in Felix Farley's *Bristol Journal* of 4 June 1836, announced a sale of 'All those valuable Mills, and works called Baptist Mills, heretofore used as Brassworks, having good waterpower, and extensive and substantial buildings capable of being applied to any manufacturing purpose. Also twenty Dwelling-Houses and cottages, and sundry Plots of building ground'. Deeds show that the site was sold piece-meal between 1836 and 1840, with the main part of the property, including the old melting and charcoal houses, being taken over by James White who later developed a pottery there. Of the remaining area, part was eventually occupied by a tanners' merchant who later built a tannery.

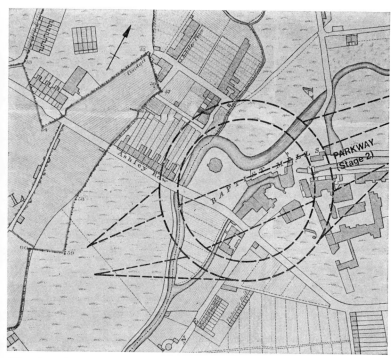

*The site of Baptist Mills compared with the M32 Parkway. Based on Ashmead's Map of Bristol drawn between 1813 and 1823, and projected position of Parkway island*

By the time that the Baptist Mills site had finally been sold, Harfords & Bristol Brass Wire & Copper Company had ceased to be a manufacturing concern in its own right. It became merely a property-owning company from 31 December 1833 when premises which remained were leased to one of the company partners, Charles Ludlow Walker, for £500 per annum.[62] Only three working mills remained, the Chew and Avon Mills at Keynsham, and the old battery mill at Saltford. The lease of Kelston Mills which was taken over from the Warmley Company was still retained at this juncture. Sited just short of Saltford on the opposite bank of the river, it completed a compact group of mills on a short stretch of the river.

Thus, the works of the old brass company, which just over thirty years before had been described as Europe's largest brass works, were now reduced to a small local concern, but still producing wares by traditional methods. With a few reductions and modifications this business was to continue trading under the name of Harfords & Bristol Brass Company for almost another hundred years.

# CHAPTER SIX

# Later Bristol Developments

'The zinc made by Mr Emerson, is whiter and brighter than any other, either English or Foreign . . . He has a patent for making Brass with Zinc and Copper; and his Brass is said to be more malleable, more beautiful, and of a colour more resembling Gold than ordinary Brass is.'

Dr Watson, Chemical Essays, 4 (1786)

AFTER the failure of the Warmley Company in 1769, the old Bristol brass works, as we have seen, took complete control of the local industry. When new concerns began to emerge the old company applied local commercial tactics similar to those it operated in Birmingham.[1] From the early 1780s, when the company was gradually deprived of its ascendancy over the country's brass production it also lost the ability to operate these price controls. It was not until then that the smaller businesses were allowed to take a significant part in the Bristol industry.

## The Champion Family

The influence of the Warmley Company was very apparent in some new developments, but little is known of William Champion's activities throughout this later period. It is possible that the methods of sulphur recovery proposed by John Champion, junior, may have been the result of collaboration within the Champion family, particularly in view of William's bankruptcy when he had been full of ideas for the expansion of Warmley.

The John Champion junior concerned with the new calcining methods, is believed to have been the son of John, nephew of

William of Warmley, a young man in his early twenties at the time
of the Anglesey negotiations. His father had withdrawn from the
Holywell business of zinc smelting and brass battery by 1765
although he continued his mining interests in various parts of
North Wales.[2] By 1774, John senior was in some kind of financial
difficulty and requesting assistance from distant members of his
family, including Sampson Lloyd.[3] This situation may have been
brought about by helping his brother William at the collapse of the
Warmley Company.

Early in 1778 John Champion, junior, wrote from Downend
House, Bristol, to Sir Nicholas Bayly, the owner of part of Parys
Mountain, to persuade him to allow Champion and his business
associates to run the part of the mine which he owned. This
suggestion was scarcely considered, but Bayly was very interested
in an additional proposal put to him concerning a new calcining
process. From subsequent correspondence, it emerges that Bayly
was about to make an agreement with Champion adopting his new
methods, and a similar agreement was also being negotiated with
the owners of territory under Thomas Williams' management.
Meanwhile, a partnership was being arranged between John Champion junior and William Roe of the Macclesfield Company, which
worked the remaining part of the mine. The new partners agreed
to pay £50 per annum to the Macclesfield Company for the right
to prepare company ores by providing a complete calcining service,
in return they were to take the benefit of the sulphur extracted by
the process.

The method improved the efficiency of subsequent smelting
processes by removing part of the sulphur content. The ore was
calcined in enclosed kilns which varied in size and shape, but those
reported in 1783 were rectangular and 40 to 50ft long. They contained hearths at regular intervals which held small amounts of
coal, and were covered by gratings and connected with one another
by horizontal brick channels. These were ventilated with draught
holes and covered over with iron plates, thus were able to draw

off fume from the burning ore in which they were completely buried. Once fired, the ore burned slowly for about six months.

When the initial water vapour had been driven off, the sulphur fume was conveyed through a horizontal flue along the ridge of the kiln through exterior flues to condensing chambers. There, the yellow powder collected to a depth of a foot or more, periodically being shovelled out and melted up in a furnace. It was then drawn off to cool and solidify in shallow cisterns and the rock sulphur which resulted was then ready for sale, mainly for making gunpowder.[4]

The year after the partnership agreement between William Roe and John Champion, junior, the process was granted Patent No 1216, on 17 March 1779, in the name of William Roe. These patent rights were probably conceded by previous arrangement, but shortly after this date, John Champion, junior, died. In August, he was buried in the graveyard of the Society of Friends at Redcliffe in Bristol, his age being recorded as 25.[5] Earlier the same year, he had been granted Letters Patent for his process of extracting tar from coal whilst preparing coke for blast furnaces, Patent No 1223, 17 May 1779. The patent requirements were not completed as no specification was ever enrolled.

Following the death of John Champion, junior, the Anglesey companies adopted his process as a means of improving their sulphurous ores. It was learned eventually, however, that the production of sulphur by this method hardly covered the costs involved, and little financial gain could have benefitted those concerned with it, or from the partnership which had been organised to make its profit solely from the sales of sulphur recovered.[6]

On 19 May 1780, William Champion advertised in *Gore's General Advertiser* of Liverpool, the sale of one-quarter share 'in the new and valuable concern of extracting brimstone from copper ore'. This may have been a family share, or that of his deceased nephew. From the advertisement, however, it is quite clear that the recovery process had already been installed in a copper works in the Bristol area where two kilns were operating, each containing 200 tons of ore.

Meanwhile, John senior had still been active in devising new methods in his own right, having patented a process in 1779, at the age of 74. This was No 1239, and was for making brass by his usual method with black jack or calamine, but in much larger crucibles which were carefully sealed 'So that there may be as little as possible of the sublimation of the lapis calaminaris or black jack escape out of them'. Subsequently 'old Champion' (which could have been either John or William) was mentioned as a possible candidate for managerial positions at the formation of the Birmingham Metal Company, and later, in the Cornish Metal Company. Nothing materialised from these suggestions, and the precise nature of their business during this period has not been discovered. William died in 1789, aged 79, but the following year his elder brother John was still active, trying to interest Matthew Boulton in his latest discovery. This concerned an 'imflammable matter' produced from pit coal, which he maintained was capable of providing a light suitable for lighthouses.[7] Considering Boulton's later connections with Murdoch in the development of coal gas, this correspondence of the 1790s with old John Champion is interesting. The latter died four years later at Pimlico at the age of 86,[8] but this did not bring an end to family involvement with the industry (page 126).

*James Emerson*

While the Champion sulphur process (page 119) was being adopted in the copper works, a new technique for making brass was being developed by James Emerson, former manager under William Champion at the Warmley Company.[9]

In 1780, when Peter Capper wrote his 'Serious Address' to the Birmingham manufacturers, he named Emerson as one of the victims of the activities of the 'Old Company'. He claimed that they had lowered the price of spelter from £74 to £48 per ton, to

Page 121   *Avon Mill, Keynsham:* (above) *taken in the 1920s from the old County Bridge;* (below) *taken from the millpond on the opposite side of the complex of buildings in 1945, showing the wiredrawing shop*

Page 122 (above) *The annealing cone, with warehouses and black-smiths' shop on the right and manager's house in the background;* (below) *the area underneath the annealing cone, with a dilley in the foreground, part of a long annealing furnace on the right, and annealing tongs hanging on the walls*

put Emerson into difficult straits after he had presumed to establish his works in opposition.[10] However, the main concern of the new works at Hanham was not merely the production of metallic zinc.

Prior to this time, it had been the custom to produce certain high-quality brasses by melting metallic zinc with copper. These were the more expensive metals, intended for use in jewellery and various kinds of ornament. Described by names such as pinchbeck, tomback, or Mannheim gold, all were brasses which contained a high percentage of copper, which today would be referred to as gilding metals.[11] The grades of brass utilised for the production of industrial and domestic wares continued to be made by the old method of smelting calamine with copper.

The cost of producing metallic zinc, said to be upwards of £40 per ton, appears to have been one barrier to the use of this metal for common brass.[12] Dressed and calcined calamine cost from £6 6s to £8 per ton, according to figures mentioned by Watson, and usually yielded between 25 and 33⅓ per cent of its own weight in the brassmaking process according to its quality.[13] At an estimated cost of about £24 per ton, this yielded metal represented a considerable saving on the cost of smelted zinc.

James Emerson may have found a way of reducing his production costs, or perhaps he had other motives for pioneering this new method of brassmaking. Peter Capper, when informing Boulton of the new development, remarked 'I cannot see what advantage can arrive to him'.[14] Nevertheless, in October 1781, Emerson enrolled his new specification under Patent No 1297 for making brass by melting metallic zinc with copper, describing his method in more detail than many of his predecessors:

> I take spelter ingots, and melt them down in an iron boiler. I then run the melted spelter through a ladle with holes in it, fixed over a tub of cold water, by which means the spelter is granulated or sholed, and it is then fit for making brass on any plan. I then mix fifty-four pounds of copper shot, about ten pounds of calcined calamine ground fine, and about one bushel of ground charcoal together. I then put into a casting pot a handful of this mixture, and upon it I

H

put three pounds of the sholed spelter. I then fill up the pot with the mixture
of copper shot, calcined calamine and ground charcoal. In the same manner I
fill eight other pots, so that fifty-four pounds of copper shot, twenty-seven
pounds of sholed spelter, about ten pounds of calcined calamine, and about one
bushel of ground charcoal, make a charge for one furnace, containing nine
pots, for making brass on my plan. My chief reason for using this small quantity
of calamine in the process is more for confining the spelter by its weight, than
for the sake of the increase arising from it; and I have frequently omitted the
calamine in the process. The pots being so filled they are respectively put into
a furnace, and about twelve hours completes the process. And from this charge
I have, on an average, eighty-two pounds of pure fine brass, fit for making ingots
or casting plates, for making brass battery wire or brass latten; and my brass
so made, as aforesaid, is of superior quality to any brass made from copper and
calamine.[15]

Emerson's own opinion of the quality of the metal produced by
his newly patented method was endorsed by his contemporaries. It
is possible that he calculated that the extra sales of this high-grade
product would cover his extra production costs. Dr Watson remarked,

His brass is said to be more malleable, more beautiful, and of a colour more
resembling gold than ordinary brass is. It is quite free from knots or hard
places, arising from iron, to which other brass is subject, and this quality, as it
respects the magnetic needle, renders it of great importance in making compasses.

One reason for the fine quality was thought to have been in the
zinc he used, which was 'whiter and brighter than any other, either
English or Foreign'.[16] In *Mathew's Complete Guide to Bristol*, published in 1794, Emerson's brass was described as the purest in the
world, 'its fine and excellent contexture and malleability cause
great demand for it among the most curious Artificers at Birmingham and other places and considerable quantities of it are exported'.

In spite of these very favourable comments, in March 1803
James Emerson was declared bankrupt, and later in that same year
his works were advertised for auction.[17] Situated at Hanham, on
the north bank of the Avon a short distance upriver from Crew's
Hole and Conham, the premises consisted of four spelter houses
with four cones, two calamine houses, one potroom, a millhouse
for grinding clay and a clayhouse, a millhouse for grinding black

jack, a brasshouse with four furnaces, a warehouse with a pot-room and counting-house over it, a calamine millhouse, a smith's shop, a pump and pumphouse, a charcoal-house and a buddle-house. All the tools and implements were put up for sale at the works, which was said to contain every requisite for carrying on the trade of brass and spelter making.[18]

Later, the site was associated with the organisations of Philip George and Christopher Pope (page 134) but the name of Emerson was still linked with the business. It seems very likely that the founder (who was aged 64 at the time of his bankruptcy) or possibly one of his descendants, was retained for a number of years in an advisory capacity.[19]

## Isaac Elton and Thomas Tyndall

From the early 1770s a new copper company started to operate within the Bristol area and there are indications that its activities were not impeded by the old Bristol brass company.[20] It was headed by Isaac Elton, a descendent of Abraham Elton of Conham, in conjunction with Thomas Tyndall. Both were partners in the Old Bank in Bristol, and several of the co-partners in the new copper company were also concerned in Bristol banking[21] (Appendix One, page 223).

The business became quickly known to the northern copper companies for, in 1778, there were references in the minutes of the Macclesfield Company to ore being offered to Tyndall & Co. Again, a year later, the Macclesfield Company recorded that they were 'Trying to get hold of a workman from Tyndall and Elton who can make Japan Copper'.[22] Japanned copper was produced by casting the refined metal and immersing it, while still hot, in a vessel of cold water. This treatment was said to form a slight coating of oxide, producing a finish which was particularly valued for the important East India market.[23]

Land tax returns appear to indicate that this company was oc-

cupying at least two sites leased to them by the old Bristol brass
company from the early 1780s. These could have been Crew's
Hole and Conham, the two works said to have been vacated by the
old company in favour of works at Warmley where coal was more
easily obtainable. From about 1781, the Elton and Tyndall company also took over a rolling mill at Woollard on the River Chew.
Formerly, the mill had been occupied by a tinplate manufacturing
company, whose partners included Messrs Reynolds and Getley,
and later, members of the Harford family who were not connected
with brass manufacture. The tinplate company still held the lease
from the Popham family when the mill was occupied by Elton and
Tyndall but, by 1783, the premises were legally assigned to the
copper company for the sum of £2,500.

By the mid 1790s, however, there were no further references to
the Elton and Tyndall copper company and, by 1796, the lease of
the Woollard rolling mill was taken over by the long-established
John Freeman & Copper Company. The site was conveniently
placed for this company, which had occupied the adjacent three
mills upstream of Woollard for the greater part of the century.[24]

### Lewins Mead and John Champion, junior

The possibility of opposition from the old Bristol brass company
may have been a factor in persuading one member of the Champion
family to concern himself, for a period, in a completely different
trade. This was at Young's cornmill at Lewin's Mead in the centre
of the city, but it was no ordinary corn-milling establishment.
Later, Champion family honour was to be vindicated by the development of these premises into a large 'manufactory' for the
production of brass and iron wire.

In May of 1783, George Watson who was still supplying 'intelligence' to Matthew Boulton in Birmingham, wrote of his visit
to the cornmill the previous week. This was

to the engine of the late Mr Wasborough in Lewins Mead, Bristol . . . at Young and Champion's Corn Mills—and [I] was surprised to see it quite altered and at full work scarcely to be heard.

I find a Mr Gough from B'ham has been down to do the Mill works with great rapidity, as the Engine with Seven foot Stroke goes 13 times a minute . . . I understand the weight is equal to 24 tons—and that the Coal it consumes is from 3 to 4 Bushells an hour—for unless it has full steam it will not work—I don't know whether I give you a proper definition, but any other particulars I could immediately learn.[25]

By making use of the flywheel and crank to convert the vertical steam-engine movement into rotary motion, Matthew Wasborough had delayed James Watt in his effort to solve the same problem. Watt was forced to employ the more elaborate device of a sun-and-planet gear to overcome existing patent rights; hence Boulton's interest in the Bristol engine, which would have been regarded as direct competition to the interests of his company. Wasborough died in 1781 at the age of 28 years, before his invention had been fully appreciated.[26]

In 1790, young John Champion (believed to be the son of William of Warmley, who had died the previous year) made contact with Matthew Boulton through his Birmingham cousin, Charles Lloyd. He wished to experiment in adapting the Wasborough engine to James Watt's separate condensing system in an attempt to reduce its running costs. The former owners had operated at considerable loss, so Charles Lloyd explained to Boulton. Lloyd also mentioned that the Champion family owned some very large warehouses at Lewins Mead, adjacent to the cornmill containing the Wasborough engine.[27] The mill had been previously leased by Champion, but soon it was to be purchased outright in readiness for the alterations.

James Watt replied to Champion's approaches, explaining that he was unable to come to Bristol in the near future, but if he could have a ground plan of the engine at Lewins Mead he would propose suitable modifications. There is no further record of correspondence during the following three years, then Champion wrote again to

Boulton and Watt giving more details of his engine which was still driving the cornmill. With a cylinder of 42in diameter, a length of stroke 6ft 6in at the cylinder and 8ft 9in at the crank, 13 strokes to the minute, the engine provided power to grind 18–20 bushels of wheat per hour. This required a coal consumption of $4\frac{1}{2}$–5 bushels per hour costing £415–75 per annum which made the operation hardly worthwhile, but Champion thought a separate condenser should save considerable quantities of coal. Later that year, Boulton and Watt made certain proposals, not detailed in available records, which were accepted by John Champion. It was at this stage that he announced his intention of erecting a rolling and slitting mill powered by the engine, to work in conjunction with the cornmill.[28]

In June 1798, John Champion, by then described as a manufacturer of brass, copper and iron wire, patented a new invention for 'An Improved Method of Making Wire from Rolled and Slit Iron, either Foreign or English, put in operation by various Powers now in Practice'. The specification made reference to established techniques in the production of brass wire,

> I then slit these pipes (either hot or cold) into threads or strings of the sizes necessary by means of metal slitters (similar to those used in the slitting of brass slips for the making of brass wire), after which I pass my strings or threads singly (either hot or cold) between metal rollers with groves of such sizes as wanted (A), to which they are conducted by hollows in metal conductors (B), and which strings are immediately received after passing the roller (A) into other hollow metal receivers or tubes (C), either curved or straight, as necessary.[29]

Shortly after obtaining this patent, John Champion advertised his Lewins Mead premises for sale by auction, to take place on 8 January 1799. The extensive property, which was described as 'a Capital Brass and Iron Wire, Copper and Lead Mills and Manufactory', had a frontage on Lewins Mead, and backed right down to the River Frome. It still contained the large steam engine, together with two brassmaking furnaces, and another for annealing, several sets of rolls and slitters, including a large pair of rolls 6ft 3in wide. Other warehouses and nearby property were also to be sold at the auction and, in a separate lot, the patent rights of the iron-wire manufacturing process.[30] Property and patent rights were bought by Philip George (page 132).

This sale appears to have marked the final exit of the Champion family as manufacturers in the Bristol brass industry, although John, or some other member of the family, may possibly have continued as partner or adviser in one of the remaining companies. In 1806, a certain John Champion was writing from Birmingham to Lord Ribblesdale to enquire if calamine was to be procured from mines on his land at Malham Moor, Yorkshire. Later, he offered £13 14s per ton for the best-quality calamine, a very high price, and also showed interest in other non-ferrous ores which he considered might be available. In further correspondence, he professed an interest in zinc manufacture, in order to take advantage of the new methods of producing brass which employed metallic zinc, commenting that Bristol was the only place where the metal was now being smelted; he had some connection with a former zinc-smelting works in the Swansea area, which he hoped to put into operation. It is not clear whether he was, by then, working on his own account or as an agent for another business, possibly the Birmingham Metal Company.[31]

The correspondence ceased after 1807 but, in 1811, a certain Mr J. Champion was declared bankrupt. It has not been possible to establish if this was John Champion of Bristol.

## The Fromebridge and Bridgwater Companies

Some twenty-five miles north of Bristol, near Frampton-on-Severn on the River Frome, John Purnell and his partners were in business at Fromebridge Mill making wire from iron. By about 1775, the premises had been greatly extended and were also utilised for brass-wire manufacture, probably being supplied with brass by the Bristol brass company.[32] The business grew and in 1796, the Macclesfield Company minuted a decision to draw its own wire to the same gauges as those employed at Bristol and Fromebridge, giving the impression that by then the Fromebridge company constituted an important factor in the industry.[33] The company continued successfully until the death of Purnell in 1805 when business dwindled, and there were financial difficulties until it ceased about 1809.

Another company of the same period, outside the Bristol area but undoubtedly connected with the city's brass industry, was the brass foundry of T. Pyke at Bridgwater, some thirty miles south. In 1881 this business was advertising, in Bristol newspapers, the sale of brass cannon said to be designed on a newly improved principle.[34] In 1786, Pike was an unsuccessful candidate for an official position in the Cornish Metal Company, together with 'Old' Champion, and George Watson. At the time he stated that he had been in the industry for over thirty years and was a consumer of a hundred tons of copper and brass per annum.[35]

In addition to these businesses there were several smaller brass foundries scattered over the area, owned by men who could best be described as craftsmen rather than manufacturers. Prior to the general adoption of the direct method of making brass by alloying metallic zinc with copper, all would have obtained their metal from a large producer, probably from the old Bristol brass company in the days of its ascendancy.

### Anderson, New & Company

At about the turn of the century, another company came into existence with a large amount of available capital. It appears, however, to have possessed rather less technical expertise than other similar Bristol businesses. Its stated purpose was the manufacture of spelter; copper, brass and brass wire; and the smelting of copper; under the name of Anderson, New & Co.

In 1806, the company was reformed, and deeds then referred specifically to the fact that the smelting of copper had not yet been achieved. The property to be taken over by the new organisation consisted of watermills, cottages, outbuildings, horses and carts, and a steam engine, at premises at Netham in the parish of St George and probably at Two Mile Hill (the name is indistinct in the relevant document) in the Parish of Bitton. Offices of the new company, now to be known as Pitt, Anderson, Birch & Company, were to continue in Redcross Street, just off Old Market. New capital was to be raised in five equal shares totalling £60,000 and, from 24 June 1807, the business to be undertaken was to include the making of spelter, copper and brass, brass wire, and the buying of lapis calaminaris, black jack, lead and other ores.[36]

There is little evidence on the success of these manufactures, but two years later the company was in the news for other reasons. On 17 August 1809, a claim came before the assizes in Gloucester, made by Messrs Pitt, Anderson, Birch & Co, against the Bristol Dock Company. They declared that their watermill premises at Netham had been rendered useless by the construction of the Floating Harbour in the dock-improvement scheme of William Jessop. The partners had already been offered £4,000 as recompense by the dock company, but maintained that they would now be forced to purchase a steam engine to replace their watermill. This would involve them in great expense in upkeep, maintenance and staff, and they therefore claimed £40,000. In cross-examination, the company admitted that the old mill had been in bad condition and frequently incapable of working, owing to the state of the tides. Subsequently, the jury awarded the company £10,000.[37]

There were further changes in the partnership in 1814, but by 1819 it had disappeared from the manufacturies listed in the local directories.

## The Philip George Company

The Bristol business of Philip George entered the field of brass manufacture in 1800, having previously been concerned only with the production of lead shot at Redcliffe Hill.[38]

For well over a century, lead shot had been manufactured in Bristol in a small-scale process by pouring the melted metal through a sieve into a vessel of water.[39] This was the process which, as already mentioned, must have inspired the granulation of copper pioneered by Nehemiah Champion. In 1782, William Watts, a plumber of Redcliffe Hill, Bristol, patented a new method of making lead shot. He continued the traditional method of pouring the metal through a sieve, but from a considerable height, thus allowing the metal to take up a spherical shape as it fell. Watts built a tower on Redcliffe Hill to carry out his successful process, and is said to have amassed a fortune, only to quickly lose it again by speculative building work. In February 1794, he was declared bankrupt and, by September of the same year, his premises in Redcliffe Hill and the right to use his patented process, were in the hands of Philip George and his Patent Shot Company.

Philip George was the elder son of William George, distiller. A younger son, James, had been connected with the start of the Bristol brewing business, and later, was to be concerned in establishing the Castle Bank. Under the care of Philip George, the Patent Shot Company developed into a flourishing business, taking full advantage of William Watt's process which produced shot of a truly spherical shape.[40]

When John Champion's wireworks came up for sale in Lewins Mead, it was Philip George who purchased it, again acquiring a patented process. In Bristol directories of 1800, George drew attention to his new wire manufactory at 70 Lewins Mead but, by 1808, similar entries were under the name of Philip George Junior & Co, Copper and Wire Manufacturers. By 1814, the company premises were stated to be in Cheese Lane, but whether these were additional premises, or whether the business had moved completely, cannot be assessed from available sources.

*Christopher Pope & Company*

By 1815, the company of Philip George Junior was advertising in local directories, that its wares included copper, spelter, wire, patent zinc and iron, thus giving some indication of a liaison with yet another company. This was the business started by Christopher Pope in 1809, with headquarters in York Street in the centre of Bristol. Directories stated that he manufactured 'Patent Malleable Zinc', and this was probably smelted at Emerson's old site at Hanham.

Prior to 1805, the only use for zinc apart from blending it in various alloys, is believed to have been for casting. It was not possible to work the metal by any processes, and it could not be described as malleable. In 1805, Charles Sylvester and Charles Hobson, of Sheffield, patented methods of hot-working zinc sheet which would undergo treatment under the hammer, and could also be drawn into wire.[41] No documentary connection has been discovered between these two men and Christopher Pope, but there must have been some agreement to enable him to advertise his production of patent malleable zinc.

From 1815, this product was marketed by the Philip George organisation, which also added iron sheet and hoops to its list of manufactures. By the early 1820s, however, the whole business was resumed under Christopher Pope. Phillip George disappeared from the directory list of manufacturers, and the patent lead-shot company was continued under the name of Christopher George, younger brother of Philip George, junior.

Just after Pope resumed control, new premises were established at Soundwell, near the site of William Champion's new copper furnaces of the 1760s. This works produced zinc and brass, and manufactured brass battery by means of nine steam-powered battery hammers. In 1823, Christopher Pope patented an alloy of zinc and tin or, alternatively, zinc, lead and tin, to be rolled into sheet metal.[42] This was intended as a material for sheathing ships, and for roofing buildings, but it probably had little practical value for the purpose of sheathing.[43] Neither does it appear to have been widely adopted as a roofing material, although zinc sheet was used

later for this purpose. Thus, the possible failure of this patent
may have been a contributary factor in Christopher Pope's bankruptcy a few years later, in 1832.[44] In the following month, his
premises at Soundwell were advertised for sale.

A little later in the year, other premises of the company were
advertised for sale, including the large rolling mill at Cheese Lane.
There, steam-powered equipment for producing hoop-iron; iron,
brass and copper wire; sheet lead; battery and sheet brass; was
all disposed of, in premises which had a frontage on Cheese Lane
and extended back towards the river.[45] Apart from the iron goods
produced, it can be seen that the company had manufactured
brassware in much the same range as the Harford & Bristol Brass
Company, but had used more modern techniques and equipment.

After the sales, the business still continued working under the
same name of Christopher Pope, for about ten years.[46] During this
time, in 1838, the Hanham zinc-smelting works, formerly belonging
to James Emerson and later associated with Philip George and
Christopher Pope, were offered for sale by auction.[47] The property
(page 124) still consisted of four spelter furnaces and 'every requisite
for manufacturing spelter', but it seems unlikely that it was ever
used again. By 1844, the business remaining under the name of
Christopher Pope had disappeared from the companies listed in the
Bristol directories.

Thus most of the Bristol companies connected with the brass
industry which had proliferated towards the turn of the century,
had eventually come under control of the Christopher Pope
organisation, which had finally ceased to exist.


*Capper Pass*

There remained, however, one business which had been established in a small way after the arrival of the Pass family from
Walsall, about 1815.[48] The elder son of the family, Capper Pass,
dealt in scrap metal, refining it at premises near the gas works in

## FREEHOLD PROPERTY.

### At *SOUND-WELL, five Miles from Bristol.*

# TO BE SOLD BY AUCTION,

### *By Mr. WALL,*

At the Sign of the Horse-Shoe, in the Parish of SISTON, (*and not at Mangotsfield as before advertised*) in the County of Gloucester, on TUESDAY, the 14th day of February next, at 1 o'clock in the Afternoon, (by Order of the Assignees of the Estate of Mr. Christopher Pope, a Bankrupt) either altogether or in separate Lots, as may be determined upon at the time of Sale,

THE following very desirable Freehold PROPERTY, viz.: All those extensive BUILDINGS, with the capital Steam-Engines set up thereon, all of which have been erected by Messrs. Christopher Pope and Company, within the last ten years, for the purpose of carrying on the Spelter and Brass Business, at an enormous expense, together with about three Acres and an half of Land, surrounding the same.

The Buildings consist of a good Dwelling-House for a foreman or manager, and a Counting-House adjoining, and also of the following Ranges, viz.:

One Range containing about 182 feet in length, 31 feet in width, and 20½ feet in height, with 4 Calciners, 2 Spelter Furnaces, and Pot-room, wherein is a ten-horse Steam-Engine, for working two pair of powerful Crushers, and calculated for doing other work.

Another Range about 120 feet long, 24 feet wide, and 9 feet high, containing a Steam-Engine of 16-horse power, in the centre, erected for working 9 brass Battery Hammers, or any other work.

Another Range about 78 feet long, 16 feet wide, and 8½ feet high, containing a Smith's Shop, Carpenters' Shop, Gig-House and Stable.

Another Range about 66 feet long, 30 feet wide, and 17 feet high, containing 2 Spelter Furnaces.

Another Range about 31 feet long, 28 feet wide, 15 feet high, having therein 3 Brass Fires with ample room for 3 more, together with cabins or sleeping places for the workmen adjoining.

Another Range about 60 feet long, 29 feet wide, and 10 feet high, containing 6 Brass Fires, with cabin or sleeping places for the workmen adjoining.

Another Range about 44 feet long, 14 wide, 6 feet high, a Warehouse for metals, &c.

The Buildings may be very easily converted into Dwelling-Houses, or a Glass-House, Pottery, Pinnery, or any other Manufactory requiring space of ground, and to which cheap coal is an object, as that article can be rendered upon the premises at a very low price.

Another material advantage incident to this Property, is its contiguity (being distant 50 feet only) to a branch of the Bristol and Gloucestershire Railway, (with which it can be united,) thereby affording a cheap and ready mode of conveyance to the River Avon, the city of Bristol and its vicinity.

For an inspection of the Property, apply to Mr. BIRT on the Premises, and for further particulars to Mr. PHILIP GEORGE, the Assignee, at the Manufactory late of Messrs. Pope and Co. Cheese-lane, St. Philip's; to Mr. LIONEL O. BIGG, Solicitor, St. Stephen-Street; or Mr. FRANCIS SHORT, Solicitor, 57, Corn-Street, Bristol.

---

*Auction sale notice from the* **Bristol Gazette**

Avon Street. The business appeared in Bristol directories in 1836, and gradually increased in size until 1840, when new premises were taken in the Bedminster district of Bristol. The recovery of scrap, or secondary metals, remained the main purpose of the enterprise, and the refining of these metals provides a link between the old eighteenth-century copper and zinc-smelting industries and those of modern times. The production of zinc developed as an entirely separate industry from brass, particularly after the mid-century, when John Lysaght's and the Bristol Ironworks became concerned in galvanising. The industry developed further in the twentieth century with the erection of the National Smelting Company's zinc smelter at Avonmouth, a site which continues to this day under the Rio Tinto-Zinc Corporation, which has now also absorbed the Capper Pass Company.[49]

## The Harfords & BBCo

Throughout the development and decline of the brass works which flourished at the turn of the eighteenth to nineteenth centuries, there still remained the two old companies, successors of the early pioneers. The John Freeman & Copper Company continued at Swinford and the River Chew mills, the Harfords & Bristol Brass Company remained in business at Saltford and Keynsham.

After the lease of the brass works to Charles Ludlow Walker at the close of 1833, new premises were erected at Avon Mill, Keynsham, known as the Upper Works.[50] This was situated well above normal flood levels and away from available water power, and it can therefore be assumed that steam power was introduced at this time, probably with a grasshopper engine (page 152). In June 1835, an advertisement suggests that new plant had been installed on the premises: 'To Metal Turners. A Sober Steady man who is capable of Working at a Lathe may hear of constant employment, by applying to Harfords B.B.Co's Brass Works, Keynsham'.[51] The man was required for the turning of pans made by the battery method, in order to give them a smooth finish. Tube manufacture was also undertaken, although it is doubtful if this was drawn, being more likely to have been joined, by the old method.

New furnaces were constructed at the Upper Works during 1834, possibly coinciding with an important change in the technique of brass production.[52] A mid-nineteenth-century account records that the company ceased to make calamine brass at about this period and subsequently brass was made at Keynsham by the new, simpler direct method of melting metallic zinc with copper which had been pioneered by James Emerson at Hanham (page 123). It had not been widely adopted immediately after the process was patented, but the 1830s brought alterations to import tarriffs, which allowed more foreign zinc into the country, lowering the price substantially.[53]

While the building of Upper Works was in progress, just over an acre of land belonging to Avon Mill was sold, enabling the construction of the Great Western Railway through the site. Another plot of land was sold at Saltford for the same purpose, and stations were later built in close proximity to both mills. At Saltford the brass workers chose to commemorate the railway by roughly incising a stone at the side of one of the annealing ovens. It still reads 'Begun Diggin the Rail Road 11 June 1836'.

1841 brought negotiations for the lease of the remaining property to be taken over by a partnership between Charles Ludlow Walker, and J. H. Vivian of the great Swansea copper-smelting concern which had developed in South Wales.[54] There had been correspondence between these two men, but there is no evidence of previous business connection.[55] The valuer employed by Vivian found that, in spite of the recent building of the Upper Works, many of the older premises together with much of the machinery and, above all, the manager's house, were all in a very bad state of repair. A value could not be settled to the mutual satisfaction of both parties, consequently the proposed partnership was eventually abandoned, leaving Walker to remain for the fourteen-year lease. This was due to expire in 1847 and by then he was reluctant to renew, only being persuaded by a reduced rent and the prospect of a new manager's house offered by the Harfords. This was built during 1852, complete with clock and bell-tower, at a cost of £643 2s 9d.[56]

The value of the watermill sites dropped rapidly during these years as the methods used in them became more outdated. There were also worries about the health of C. L. Walker, and from various reports it is apparent that the Harfords were trying to sell the property from about 1855.

An auction sale of the whole works as a going concern was advertised to take place on 17 July 1859.[57] It was not a good time to dispose of the property, as in February of that same year the lease of the Freeman & Copper Company mill at Swinford, had been relinquished, and their machinery sold.[58] As may well have been expected, no sale arose from this first auction of the Harford property and, when the Walker lease became due to expire again early in 1862, the company arranged a second auction, this time with no reserve on the price. Efforts were still being made to sell by private treaty up to July after the auction, when an offer of £3,650 was made for all three remaining mills, and was eventually accepted.[59]

The new company was a partnership between Alexander Stead, Henry Elford, and Donald and David Bain. The Bains were the principal partners, who eventually took over the shares owned by Elford and Stead. Donald Bain had been concerned in the Swansea copper-smelting industry, and still intended to continue trading under the name of the Harfords & Bristol Brass Company.[60]

The Bains appear to have been rather proud of the ancient traditions and methods of working. In the 1870s the old battery mill at Keynsham ceased to be part of the works but the Avon and Saltford mills continued, completely outdated, but still producing good-quality wares. The limited modernisation introduced during this period was mainly for continuing production by the traditional methods. Although a later steam engine and more modern annealing

Page 139 (above) *Waterwheels Nos 4 and 5, the only pair housed together at Avon Mill, both 18ft dia;* (below) *this sluice arrangement was typical of all eight waterwheels at Avon Mill*

Page 140    (above) *The wiredrawing shop of the lower works,*
*Avon Mill;* (below) *the Top Yard from the opposite side of*
*Keynsham weir*

ovens were installed in the works, the eight waterwheels still remained the main source of power at Avon Mill.

In a letter of 1879, Donald Bain claimed to be one of the largest manufacturers of pin wire in the country. He was then using steam power for drawing tubes, and had numerous shoe-rivet machines operated by water power, installed at Avon Mill. The market available within the extensive boot and shoe industry in the Kingswood area of Bristol was the reason for this particular process. Wiredrawing and battery production were continued by traditional methods and no methods of spinning or pressing hollow-ware vessels were ever introduced.[61]

The Bains were also responsible for planting the surroundings of Avon Mill with ornamental and forest trees. A vine was trained over the wire shops situated at the edge of the millpond, providing a pleasant scene from the manager's house in the mill grounds.

In 1874, efforts were made to increase the efficiency of the Avon Mill waterwheels, raising the height of Keynsham weir by adding metal plates to the rear of the structure. The legal right to carry out this alteration had to be obtained from the next mill upstream, whose waterwheels were liable to be fouled by the extra height of water. In 1902, a payment of £315 was made to the owners of Swinford Mill to retain this right perpetually.[62] Donald Bain died in 1903 and the ownership of the business then passed to others in his family. Its management came more completely under the control of A. T. Davies, formerly a Cornish mining engineer, who had been at Avon Mill since the 1880s.

With the intense competition from modern industry, orders had begun to decline prior to the twentieth century. To combat expense, steam power was only used when the floods put the waterwheels out of action.

During World War I, the works became busy once again, mainly producing brass plates for shells. Soon after hostilities ceased a small amount of new work was available in the production of high-quality plates to be engraved for war memorials. A market still

I

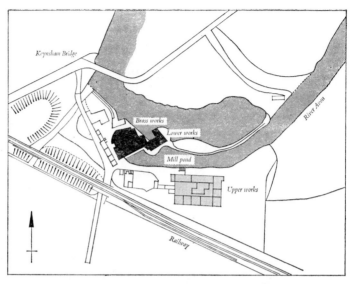

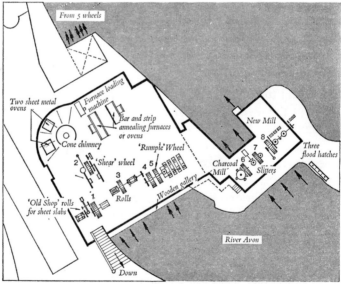

*A sketch map of Avon Mill works, Keynsham*

existed to supply brass for engraving shop-front nameplates, particularly the brass sills once fitted at the base of plate-glass windows, but these were fast going out of fashion. Makers of musical brass instruments bought supplies of quality sheet-metal from the Keynsham and Saltford mills, but these outlets were not sufficient and men soon began to be laid off again. In 1925, after the death of F. D. Bain, nephew of Donald Bain, the old mill at Saltford was sold, and by the end of the same year A. T. Davies took over ownership of the remaining Avon Mill, with his son, A. C. V. Davies, as manager.

This arrangement lasted for less than two years for, in June 1927, Avon Mill was conveyed to Messrs E. S. & A. Robinson, paper manufacturers, after just over 220 years in the Bristol brass industry.[63]

# CHAPTER SEVEN

# The Old Mills: Work and Workers

'All the principal buildings and a great part of the machinery are in a state of general decay.'

Surveyor's Report (1841)

As the two mills at Keynsham and Saltford struggled on into the twentieth century, their difficulties increased. Competition from the mass-producing industry in the Midlands became more intense as time passed, and its lower prices captured many of the markets which the west-country business had traditionally held.[1]

The Midlands industry continued to modernise as the old water-powered equipment of the Harford company became more decrepit but in the last fifty years of its existence, much of this equipment was unique in the British Isles. As such, it is of great interest to the industrial historian. For many stages of brass manufacture, the methods used were still basically those of the eighteenth century with a few modern adaptions, but the skill and ingenuity of both men and management kept the high reputation for quality which the business had always enjoyed.

*Brass Melting*

When Avon Mill closed in 1927, it had contained for over a century the heart of the industrial complex that was the Harfords & Bristol Brass Company.[2] Here, brass metal was produced.

No information has been discovered on the methods used here to make calamine brass, the process abandoned in the 1830s; but the Keynsham version of the direct method which took its place was simple enough. The basic materials were refined copper and metallic zinc (or spelter as it was always called by the men), together with with scrap brass of high quality.[3] At Avon Mill, much of the copper in later years came from scrap sources too, particularly from old Atlantic cable. Zinc must have been obtained from sources outside the company as the Warmley zinc-smelting furnaces had been relinquished in the 1830s.[4] Scrap brass, or shruff, came from the offcuts of various processes, carefully saved and returned to the melting house and was also purchased from outside sources. Samples were carefully tested and sorted, to ensure the highest quality and to enable the correct percentages of copper to zinc to alloyed in the finished metals.[5]

The responsibility of balancing raw materials correctly was assigned to the mixer, an experienced man who kept numerous notebooks of percentage figures. These gave details of the various qualities of scrap and virgin metals necessary to produce the desired types of brass. The notebooks were unfortunately destroyed in quite recent years,[6] but it is not difficult to imagine the kinds of metal produced at Keynsham. Best Yellow Brass, or cartridge brass as it was often called, theoretically 70 per cent copper to 30 per cent zinc, was the alloy normally used when brass was required for subjection to severe mechanical treatment. Such processes as cold rolling, wiredrawing and battery work all come within this category, and it was in all this work that the company particularly specialised. In practice, the analyses of the metal of locally owned utensils known to have been made at the mills show some deviation from the optimum figures. However, the percentages of copper to zinc all fall within the range of alpha brasses, containing up to 37 per cent zinc, which are characterised by good ductility and formability so essential to the normal work at Keynsham.[7]

Other grades of brass outside this range, were possibly produced for selling to brassfounders and other branches of the industry, even for the occasional sand castings produced in the melting house at the Top Yard. Such metals would have included higher proportions of zinc to copper, making them much cheaper to produce, but this output must have been only of secondary importance.

All the melting was carried out at the Top Yard where the large metal stores were situated. Here also was a series of Birmingham single-pot furnaces, about 10in square by 2ft deep, used only for the occasional work of casting which was not part of the firm's normal commercial production. Such facilities, although only sporadically used, explain the existence of several small cast ornaments which are treasured in the homes of many Saltford and Keynsham families which have been connected with the mills.[8]

Most of the melting took place in the four traditional beehive furnaces, two of which were kept constantly in use. In these, the plumbago crucibles, eight to a furnace, were brought to red heat before receiving the copper and brass scrap to be melted. When the copper was just on the point of melting, zinc was added gradually, lump by lump, with great care. Some zinc was always lost by the volatilisation which immediately occurred, and this loss had to be allowed for in the mixer's calculations. The dense fumes and flame as the zinc oxidised made it necessary for the melters to protect themselves with cloths across their mouths and noses. As soon as the metal was fully melted, it was skimmed and poured into cast-iron moulds, previously prepared by warming, lightly oiling, and then dusting with powdered charcoal.

The moulds were made in two halves, held together with bands driven on to slightly tapering exteriors. Different moulds produced ingots of metal of the shapes most suited to their intended purpose. For example, slips only $4\frac{1}{4}$in wide by $1\frac{1}{4}$in by 84in long were produced for making wire; slabs of varying sizes, from 12in by $2\frac{1}{4}$in by 24in, to 12in by 1in by 36in, were for rolling into brass sheet.[9]

From the total output of brass made at Keynsham, some was sold as metal, through the trade; but this was a very small proportion compared with the earlier years of the industry. Once the direct method of making brass had been adopted universally, small businesses could easily produce their own requirements, where previously they had been obliged to buy supplies from the few large companies making calamine brass.[10] In consequence, this development deprived the Keynsham works of a large part of its previous market. From the latter half of the nineteenth century, almost all the metal produced at Top Yard was intended for works manufacture in the rolling, wire or battery mills.

*Annealing*

All these processes throughout the works subjected the brass to severe mechanical treatment, which distorts the crystal structure of the metal making it hard and brittle. Further working could cause the metal to crack and to prevent this happening, heating to 500° to 600° C is required, which softens or anneals the brass; work can then proceed to the next stage.[11] Frequent annealing processes were required at all stages of work in the mills.

The main annealing furnaces at Keynsham were housed beneath the cone at the lower works (plates, pages 122 and 142). It seems doubtful if this large structure was originally intended for this purpose, and it has been suggested that it must have been built for the large-scale production of calamine brass when Keynsham took over this work at the closure of Baptist Mills. However, no information on this use of the cone has been discovered and, within living memory, only annealing furnaces have been in position. These were muffle furnaces, with heat from coal fires at one end being taken through flues over a barrelled roof through two openings which discharged into the cone. They were loaded at the end away from the fires, with open-sided trolleys pushed into place from a turntable. Brass slabs and sheets were placed on end in the trolley, separated by paring of scrap metal and covered with shruff sheet. Coils of wire were stacked in trays on a killot or three-legged stand. Long lengths of strip, and slip for wire production, needed to be coiled for annealing in these furnaces and were usually referred to as curls.

After each fire, when the metal had been brought to the required heat, the work was extracted from the furnaces being carefully handled with tongs, for at this stage it was easy to take a piece of metal right out of a thin sheet of brass if the tongs gripped too tightly. It was then distributed around the cast-iron flooring in order to cool as quickly as possible. The thinner sheets were ready for working in about a quarter of an hour.

Strip brass of up to 34ft in length could be accommodated without coiling in two fairly modern furnaces, one 30ft long, the other 34ft, both installed in the area under the cone. Other smaller furnaces for annealing were also to be found at Top Yard.[12]

The very much older furnaces still remaining at Saltford and Kelston appear to date from the eighteenth century, probably developed from the coal-fired annealing furnaces patented by the Champions.[13] Whereas Nehemiah Champion's furnace patented in 1723 held containers which had to be smeared with clay to protect the contents from furnace gases, the furnace remains which still exist had their linings smeared with clay, making containers unnecessary. No furnace details are included in the part of William Champion's patent of 1767 which refers to annealing, but he was responsible for building Kelston in the late 1760s. At this site, only the shells of two furnaces still survive, two tall tapering squared stacks, with open arches at either side of each base, basically the same in overall measurement and design as those still at Saltford which contain more of the interior structure. These were muffle furnaces, similar in principle to those under the cone at Avon Mill. They were loaded at one archway, and two coal fires extending along either side of the chamber were tended from the archway at the opposite end. Heat and gases were drawn up in wide cavities on both sides of the chamber and discharged through flues into the tall squared chimney.

The massive firebrick-lined door of each furnace ran in guides on the inner surface of the stonework, and was counterbalanced by weights in a wooden box, carried on a pivotted horizontal beam.

# Saltford annealing furnace reconstructed from the visible remains January 1973

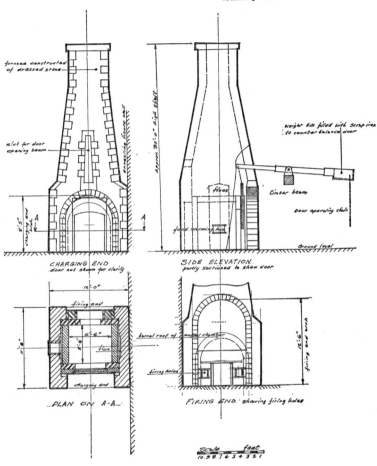

A weighted lever of this type survives at the Saltford Mills showing how the arrangement enabled the furnace door to be opened quite easily, by pulling the weighted box down with a length of light chain. A long vertical slit in the stonework of the stack accommodated the movement of the wooden beam, and is a noticeable feature of the Kelston stacks (plates, page 87).

Great care had to be taken by the men to ensure that no injurious sulphur-bearing fumes could enter the interior of the furnace to affect the quality of the brass. They were responsible for blocking any likely gaps with fire-clay kept on hand for this purpose. Experience was also needed to prevent the furnace from getting too hot, particularly at the final annealing of completed work, when the temperature was taken to a higher degree than in the previous stages and there was a danger of the brass starting to melt.

The annealing process caused the surface of the metal to oxidise, or scale, and it was essential that this should be removed before further processing. The brass was immersed in lead-lined troughs containing vitriol and water, ie a dilute solution of impure sulphuric acid, with about ½gal of acid added to 10gal of water. The metal was then thoroughly washed in clean running water and carefully dried in bran, ready for the next stage in manipulation.[14]

### Sources of Power

All the manipulative processes were still being powered by waterwheels at both Keynsham and Saltford in the final years of the mills. The only exception came when flooding stopped the wheels turning. Then the steam plant at Keynsham's Top Yard came into use, being above the normal floodline. This was a part of the works constructed in 1834 and originally known as Upper Works (see page 137).

The older part of the works at river level was powered by eight undershot waterwheels, of varying sizes and construction. Each wheel was supplied with water from a hatch, or sluice, that was raked at an angle, typical of many undershot wheels in the Bristol area (plate, page 139).

## Avon Mill Waterwheels[15]

| Wheels | Equipment driven | Special features |
|---|---|---|
| No 1<br>18ft dia by 3ft 4in | A pair of breaking-down rolls, or alternatively, a pair of finishing rolls | The Old Shop rolls, driven through cast-iron gearwheel with inserted wooden teeth, and a 15 ton flywheel |
| No 2<br>16ft dia by 2ft 1in | Two pairs of shears, a grindstone, force pump, lathes, a rod-straightening machine and other special machines | Wheel badly stressed by intermittent load of shears. Bolt holes worn and all equipment loose. Refitted 1912 |
| No 3<br>18ft dia by 2ft 10in | The lower roll of main rolling mill; alternatively, a heavy slitting mill, or heavy groove rolls | Lower roll driven direct. Shaft replaced in 1917 |
| No 4<br>18ft dia by 2ft 10in | The upper roll of main rolling mill | Geared to drive in opposite direction to lower roll by spur wheels of 79 and 80 teeth |
| No 5<br>18ft dia by 3ft 10in | The main wiredrawing plant | The rumple wheel, housed with No 4. |
| No 6<br>18ft 11in dia by 2ft 3in | Charcoal-grinding mill; 2 or 3 pairs of horizontal grindstones used alternatively. Had once driven shoe rivet-heading machines | In later years this wheel and its equipment was little used |
| No 7<br>13ft 6in dia by 2ft 10in | Standard slitting mill. Had once driven edge-runners preparing crucible fire-clay | Bevel wheels and heavy vertical shaft to slitting mill, with teeth on alternate gears of beech |
| No 8<br>18ft dia by 2ft 10in | Upright rolls for wire preparation and other wiredrawing equipment | The New Mill. Upright rolls driven by high-increase spur gears |

The Top Yard steam plant drove equipment which duplicated that found in the lower works to a very large extent. A 10hp grasshopper steam engine had once been installed here, possibly at the time that the yard was being built in 1834, but this was replaced in 1881 when an effort was being made to expand the works to counteract opposition from the Midlands industry. Undoubtedly, this steam plant had been used to its full extent at some time, but not within living memory. It was cheaper to use water power.

When the grasshopper engine was replaced in 1881, a large Lancashire boiler was installed, with two engines to power the rolling and wiredrawing processes. The rolling-mill engine was 90hp, 48rpm single-cylinder condensing, with a 15 ton flywheel, and a slide valve on top of the cylinder. It drove one pair of rolls for producing sheet, and a narrower pair of slip rolls for the preparation of long narrow strip used for the production of wire. The wire-mill engine was 40hp, originally a single-cylinder slide-valve, which was later converted by adding another engine, so that the two worked on the same crankshaft. This drove 2 small pairs of slip rolls, and 44 wiredrawing benches in two groups of 15 and 29 arranged in separate shops. In addition, the same engine powered a rod-drawing bench, a rotary rod-straightener, a lathe and other special machinery, all rarely used in the later years except when the lower works were flooded.[16]

Saltford Mills had no alternative source of power in times of flood. Its equipment could only be driven by water, and was typical of many mills in the local industry which had been closed down before it. In 1862, the works had five wheels powering its rolling and battery mills. Two wheels, both 15ft by 3ft 6in, drove two separate sets of battery mills, each with three hammers. A further two wheels of similar size drove rolling mills and a fifth, smaller, wheel powered a grindstone.[17]

Subsequently, there were several alterations to the Saltford plant, with the wheels being utilised for various purposes, until 1908 when the battery work ceased. The small grindstone wheel remained but, by 1925, when the mill finally closed, only two of the larger wheels were working, powering the remaining rolling equipment.[18]

## Rolling

The cold rolling of slab and slip moulds to sheet, strip or bar was the first phase of works manufacture; the start of all the manipulative processes which the company normally undertook. It is therefore hardly surprising to find that plant for rolling had at one time or other been installed at almost all the mills which the company had ever owned.

At Keynsham, down at the lower works, the powerful Old Shop rolls were in constant use producing latten, or brass, sheet, driven by the No 1 wheel, and geared through a 15 ton flywheel of 18ft diameter. Only the lower roll of the pair was actually powered, allowing the top roll to lift as the thickness of metal was taken, or nipped. These were the breaking-down rolls, receiving thick slabs of metal cast in the melting shop. The work was heavy for the men, as each slab weighed about 1cwt and, after each pass, had to be manhandled over to the front of the rolls again, ready to repeat the process.[19]

Strip of 12in width was quite often produced, which merely required the 12in wide slabs to be rolled straight ahead. Under the rolls, the metal could only gain substantially in length; the width would spread just enough to allow trimming to size when the brass had been worked down to the required gauge.

The main production on this plant, however, was standard-sized sheet, and the first operation was to take the slabs to a length of 6ft. They were then cut by shears across the width, into pieces just over double the required weight of the finished sheets. After annealing, further rolling and annealing took the sheets to a width of just over 2ft, allowing for trimming then, by turning at right-angles, the length was rolled to 6ft. The sheets were then pickled to brighten the metal and inspected for shab, or marks on the surface caused by impurities or by bad mixing in the melting shop. Such marks were carefully removed by chipping them out with a chisel. Small marks in the later stages were removed by a pritchel, a pointed tool specially kept for the purpose.

After further annealing, the sheets were sprung by folding the length over in two, and then the doubled sheet was flattened. With more annealing, rolling and final removal of shab, the doubled sheets were rolled, folded-end first, to a length of 4ft on the finishing rolls. These were powered by the same wheel but, not needing to be driven through the flywheel, were situated on the opposite side of the waterwheel, away from the Old Shop rolls.

With the last stage of rolling complete, the metal was marked with a pritchel to a patterned size, and trimmed by the shears at the rear of the rolls. The doubled sheets, 2ft by 4ft, were separated in two, and ready for sale to industry and trade.

The output of standard sheet was produced to order by size and gauge, some was finished bright by pickling but most was left dull to meet the main requirements. Many special orders were taken which required their own techniques of manufacture in order to supply the customer's needs.[20]

Brass rolled for further manipulation in the works was largely produced on the main rolling mill at the lower works, or else at Saltford Mills. These rolling mills were powered differently from the Old Shop rolls, with both upper and lower rolls driven by separate wheels. At Saltford the plant included breaking-down and finishing rolls, for sheet and strip production. The bottom rolls of both sets were driven by the same wheel, whilst the top rolls, of necessity geared to revolve in the opposite direction, were powered by a similar but separate wheel. Of course it was only possible to use one set at a time, even then the wheels were heavily loaded.

On occasions, the breaking-down rolls would jam when the sheet was too thick for the adjustment made, or when perhaps the top end of a slab had spread over the top of a mould and had been allowed through the rolls without being trimmed. The wheel would thus be held fast against the great force of water, and only quick action could prevent damage. The rolls were released as quickly as possible by means of a large spanner kept specially for the purpose.

The main rolling mill at Keynsham lower works was quite simple compared with equipment at Saltford, just one pair of 13in diameter breaking-down rolls, with bottom and top rolls powered by separate wheels, Nos 3 and 4. This set worked almost continuously, producing strip from $\frac{1}{2}$in to $\frac{5}{8}$in thick for slitting into rods. It also prepared most of the works production of slip, ie the $4\frac{1}{4}$ strip, rolled to about 110ft in length, used for preparing wire. This was coiled after its last pass through the rolls, to make its great length more convenient to handle in the annealing furnace.[21]

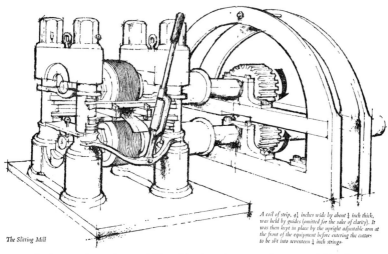

A coil of strip, 4¼ inches wide by about ¼ inch thick, was held by guides (omitted for the sake of clarity). It was then kept in place by the upright adjustable arm at the front of the equipment before entering the cutters to be slit into seventeen ¼ inch strings.

The Slitting Mill

*The slitting mill at Avon Mill. This drawing and the three following were produced from sketches made from memory in 1941 by the last manager of the mills, Mr A. C. V. Davies. Complete accuracy on small detail cannot therefore be guaranteed*

### Slitting and Rounding

Brass rod was cut from the strip by the heavy slitting mill, driven by the No 3 wheel. The equipment consisted of two spindles one above the other, revolving at about 5rpm in opposite directions as in a rolling mill. On both spindles were mounted a row of circular cutting discs, of about 13in diameter, with the top set adjusted to meet with the bottom, so forming a pair of revolving shears.

The cutting discs of the slitters had to be swaged or reshaped at regular intervals, making them thicker close up to the cutting edge to give clearance to the main body of the disc. This skilful but tiring and tedious job was originally carried out by one of the men by hand, until the manager, A. C. V. Davies, devised a means of mechanising the work. This consisted of a machine-driven hammer giving 640 blows per minute. Each blow equalled the impact of that previously made by hand, which work-hardened the edge of the disc and provided one of the more modern refinements of Avon Mill.

The discs were separated on the spindles by spacing collars according to the width of the rod required, normally $\frac{1}{2}$ to $\frac{5}{8}$in square. The rods could then be rounded if necessary by passing them through a set of grooved rolls which were also powered by the No 3 wheel, and drawn to the diameter required on the slow heavy drawbench in the wireshop, capable of taking rod of up to $\frac{5}{8}$in.

The steam-powered slitters installed in Top Yard were seldom used, but the slitting mill driven by No 7 wheel was in frequent use preparing coils of slip to a stage nearer the wiredrawing process. Here the coil of $4\frac{1}{4}$in wide strip was brought to the correct position by guides as it uncoiled and entered the slitters, to be split into 17 strings, or strips, each $\frac{1}{4}$in wide. As the row of 17 strings left the machine, travelling at about 15ft per minute, they were guided into 2 different layers. Each alternate string was deflected either upwards or downwards by a steel comb attachment, thus making

Page 157 (above) *The wharf alongside a small warehouse which housed the tailwater culverts of the waterwheels, used to overlook the old County Bridge until the floods of July 1968; (below) a row of warehouses and other ancillary buildings which still remain at Avon Mill*

Page 158  (above) *The men at Keynsham brass mills, taken about 1870 at Top Yard;* (below) *the indenture apprenticing John Varoy (later known as Fray) to Nehemiah Champion in 1745*

it possible to separate the strings more easily. The two outer strings on each edge of the strip were discarded straight away and sent to the melting house as scrap. Without further annealing, the remaining 15 strings immediately entered the upright rolls powered by the No 8 wheel.

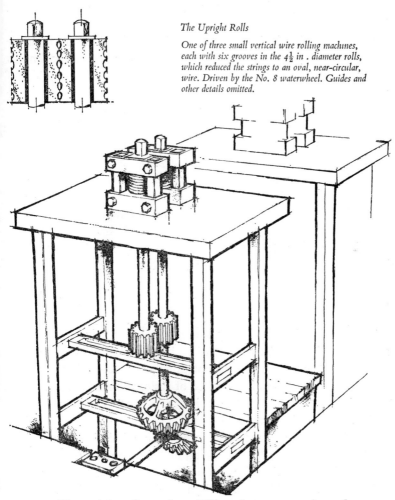

*The Upright Rolls*

*One of three small vertical wire rolling machines, each with six grooves in the $4\frac{1}{2}$ in . diameter rolls, which reduced the strings to an oval, near-circular, wire. Driven by the No. 8 waterwheel. Guides and other details omitted.*

*The upright rolls at Avon Mill used to prepare wirestock*

K

This equipment consisted of 3 small vertical wire-rolling machines, each with 6 grooves in the pairs of $4\frac{1}{2}$in diameter upright rolls. Both rolls of each of the 3 sets were driven at high speed by means of coupled spur gears on the upright shafts, and their grooves reduced the strings to an oval, almost circular, wire. A 90ft string produced 100ft of wire stock ready for the drawing-benches.

Once the string had been entered into the machine through the guides, the upright rolls were self-feeding, as long as slight tension was maintained to prevent the lengths from becoming tangled. If this was likely to occur at any point, however, the process could be stopped instantly.

The whole wire production at Avon Mill depended on these three grooved upright-roll machines, and inevitably they always revolved for as long as water permitted the No 8 wheel to turn. The whole unit powered by this wheel was known as the New Mill, although it is believed to have been installed by the early part of the nineteenth century. Several attempts are known to have been made to copy this equipment in Birmingham, but the technique met with little success elsewhere, and is believed to have been unique to the Avon Mill at Keynsham.

*Wiredrawing*

The oval-sectioned wire stock was coiled on leaving the upright rolls, and taken to the Top Yard to be annealed. There the coils were stacked in trays held by killots, ready for placing in the ovens. Afterwards they had to be cleansed of scale, washed in clean water, and dried in bran. From this point the real work of wiredrawing could start, down at the lower works.

Wiredrawing consisted of a succession of similar operations, each of which involved a wire being pulled through a tapered hole, thus gradually diminishing its section. The hole was one of a series placed in a block of carbon steel called the die block, or

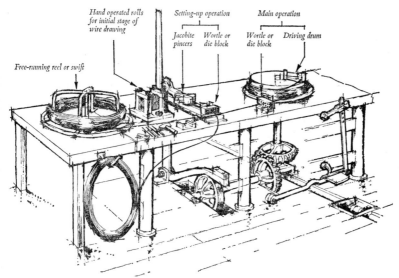

Hand operated rolls
for initial stage of
wire drawing

Setting-up operation

Main operation

Jacobite    Wortle or
pincers     die block

Wortle or    Driving drum
die block

Free-running reel or swift

*A wiredrawing bench as used at Avon Mill, Keynsham*

wortle plate. The first of these stages drew the oval wire-stock to a fully rounded rumple, as the heaviest wire was called, but although the process worked well enough when fully in operation, it required careful setting up to enable the stock to run through the smaller diameter hole. This was achieved by first of all hammering the end of the wire, reducing it enough to enter a small hand-operated set of rolls, in the centre of the bench. A short length was rolled, small enough to be inserted in the die-hole about to be used, and this length was then pulled through the hole to draw it more accurately to size. This stage was carried out by a special pair of tongs or nippers, called jacobites, worked with a reciprocating movement. They pulled back, tightly gripping the end of the wire, then the hold was released whilst the jaws moved forward again, to slip over the length pulled through the wortle. The process was repeated at some 22 to 24 pulls to the minute, until the length of wire drawn by this means was sufficient to set up the main operations.

To ease the next stage, the coils were immersed first of all in a brass pan full of soft soap solution, then the oval wirestock was placed on a free-running reel or swift, on the left of the rumple bench. From here, the short length prepared by the jacobite was passed through the required hole of a separate wortle plate, nesting against two pegs in the centre of the bench. The wire was then extended to a drum on the right of the bench, and firmly secured, screwed down by a pair of nippers. Once the drive was engaged by lowering the drum to the top of the shaft, the drum revolved at 32rpm, powered by No 5 rumple wheel, with the drive transmitted under the flooring.

Whilst the main rumpling operation was carried on, the next reel of wire stock was being prepared, on the hand-operated rolls, separate wortle plate, and jacobite, all positioned out of the way of the main operation. The jacobite was also driven from the rumple wheel, operated by an eccentric, through a curved lever and upright shaft through the centre of the bench. The jaws were coupled to the lever by links, which provided the tightening and loosening action, as the unit moved backwards and forwards.

Without further annealing, the same operation was carried out again, through a smaller hole in the same wortle plate. This reduced the diameter of the wire still further, and it was then necessary to anneal, pickle, wash and dry again, before the coil was passed on to a faster rumple bench, with the drum running at 40rpm. Here further drawing through another two holes in a wortle plate reduced the wire again.

There were eight rumple benches on the ground floor, of cast-iron construction, with all equipment driven by the No 5 water-wheel, the rumple wheel, which provided power also for the large number of wooden benches situated on the floor above.

Each unit of equipment complete on each bench was referred to as a block, and was identified by the diameter of the drum driving it. These drums decreased in size as they increased in speed with the smaller gauges of wire. Thus from the 22in diameter

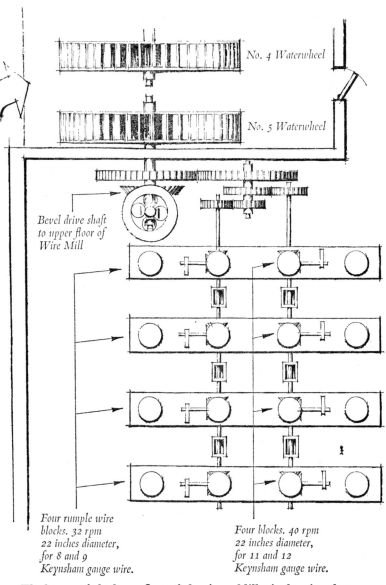

No. 4 Waterwheel

No. 5 Waterwheel

Bevel drive shaft
to upper floor of
Wire Mill

Four rumple wire
blocks. 32 rpm
22 inches diameter,
for 8 and 9
Keynsham gauge wire.

Four blocks. 40 rpm
22 inches diameter,
for 11 and 12
Keynsham gauge wire.

**The layout of the lower floor of the Avon Mill wiredrawing shop**

drums driving the rumple blocks downstairs, known as the 22in blocks, the coils progressed upstairs to equipment used for finer wires. Apart from a few assorted sizes used for non-standard wires on the upper floor, the main equipment comprised 6 blocks at 11in, 9 blocks at 9in, and 12 at 7in, producing the finest wires of all. Wires of all gauges were also produced on the upper floor of the New Mill, with all the equipment driven by the latter's water-wheel. There, with 24 blocks in all, 8 were for heavy wires from 16in to 9in, and there were 16 light blocks of 7in, producing wire for pins and the finest wires. The latter block size of 7in, was the actual diameter of the driving drum; invariably, for some unknown reason, it was called a 6in block.

In the later stages, as the wires got finer, and the reels lengthened, one man was able to attend to two blocks, or three on the last operation of all. It was then necessary to anneal, pickle, wash and dry between each hole size, compared with the two-holed working of the rumpling blocks, but otherwise each separate operation was performed in a very similar way. The diameter of wire was carefully controlled by using a die-hole only once. Before another wire was drawn through that hole, the wortle plate was removed from the pegs, and the wiredrawer peened the hole over with a hammer. He would then re-open it accurately to size with a pritchel, a rounded tool with a tapering point, by inserting it in the hole to exactly the right depth. This was done by experience, without need for any measurement.

At the final process with the finest wires it was impossible to hammer the end and handroll a short length by way of preparation for the jacobite stage. Instead, these wires were heated gently in a gas flame, and gradually pulled until two finely pointed ends were formed. The point was inserted through the wortle and the last main operation could proceed.

As the coils of wire were finished to the gauges required, they were packed for dispatch to the customer, still carrying the characteristic smell left by the soft-soap lubricant. A feature of the reels sent from Keynsham was the proper cast of the wire. A reel could be opened at any point to form a separate coil, without any fear of it tangling. At times, when production was seriously delayed by prolonged periods of winter flooding, the works tried to keep their customers supplied by buying wire from other manufacturers, and rewinding it to their special cast. This led to such widespread complaints of the quality provided, that the practice had to be stopped.

To supply larger reels of continuously joined wire, brazing, and later, during the 1890s, arc welding, was adopted to enable the works to compete with the rolled wire produced by the modern Birmingham industry. But, if Keynsham was unable to match the output, speed and low cost of the Birmingham manufacturers, there was no difficulty in producing a quality product. The high standard of the normal wire production brought regular orders from the best British firms, including other manufacturers of wire. When they needed to supply top-quality grades, Birmingham firms often bought their supplies from the Keynsham water-driven mills, but the more efficient methods of the competitors eventually lowered prices beyond the point where this unique production could possibly continue.[22]

*Batteryware*

Large quantities of brass were sold at the various stages of operation, but wire and batteryware were the two final products at the end of a long production line.

When the properties passed to the new partnership after the 1862 sale, the equipment described was much the same as it had been in 1830.[23] Attempts at modernising the ancient machinery at the Saltford battery mill were undertaken during the Donald Bain period of ownership. Thus, in 1881, a new set of battery hammers was installed, based on plant working in the Birmingham area which made greater use of wrought and cast iron in construction.

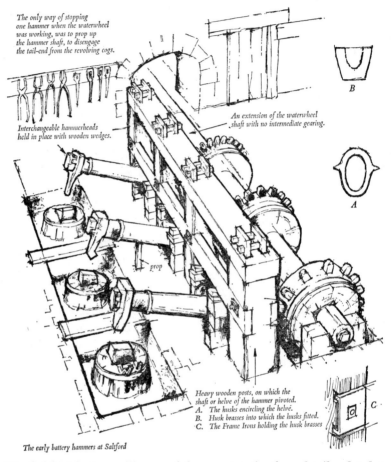

*The only way of stopping one hammer when the waterwheel was working, was to prop up the hammer shaft, to disengage the tail-end from the revolving cogs.*

*Interchangeable hammerheads held in place with wooden wedges.*

*An extension of the waterwheel shaft with no intermediate gearing.*

B

A

*prop*

*Heavy wooden posts, on which the shaft or helve of the hammer pivoted.*
*A. The husks encircling the helvé.*
*B. Husk brasses into which the husks fitted.*
*C. The Frame Irons holding the husk brasses*

C

*The early battery hammers at Saltford*

*The Saltford battery mill; an artist's reconstruction from details related to the author*

A heavy wrought-iron shaft from the waterwheel carried three cog-wheels as in the previous equipment, but the cogwheels were now made of cast iron instead of wood. They revolved, striking the hammers, which pivoted in short cast-iron frames in place of the heavy wooden posts which had previously housed the hammer bearings.[24] Robbed of the flexibility of the old wooden mechanisms, the whole plant vibrated to such an extent that it was impossible to persuade the men to use it. After several attempts at modification had failed, it was eventually abandoned in favour of the traditional plant made predominantly of wood.

A more successful alteration took place a few years later when only one of the two sets of battery plant remained, powered by a wheel 15ft diameter by 3ft 6in. Its immense wooden shaft, which carried the three large wooden cogwheels, transmitted power to three hammers by direct drive in the traditional way. This water-wheel was successfully replaced by one of 18ft diameter, mounted on a hexagonal cast-iron shaft, 20ft by 2ft across the flats, with a 6in hole through the centre. It carried 3 cast-iron cogwheels about 4ft diameter, with up to 20 wooden inserted teeth, and revolved at about 18rpm. The remainder of the hammer plant was unchanged from the original wooden construction.[25]

The battery hammers used at Saltford were tilt hammers with heads, which were frequently changed, held in place by wooden wedges on the heavy beechwood shafts, or helves. The helves were pivotted unequally, 1ft 6in from the driven end, on a husk, an oval iron band with trunnions which pivoted in brass cups mounted on tall stout wooden posts. The descending wooden cogs struck the helve forcibly down on to a sunken rebound plate. The resulting powerful, but very rapid, strokes of the hammer, permitted a vertical movement to the head of only about 3in to 3¼in, although this could be adjusted for special needs. The blows were directed on to an anvil sunk in a large iron-bound piece of tree trunk buried in the floor. Many different weights and sections of hammer heads were employed for the different stages of pan production. It was essential that they should hit the anvil absolutely square, otherwise the brass pan being worked was liable to be damaged, or dance out of control.

The normal method of stopping the hammers was by means of a stulch, a tough piece of wood about 30in long, with stout iron ferrules on each end. This was quickly thrust under the rear part of the ascending hammer helve, and held it away from the revolving cogwheel.

The function of the three hammers was the raising of brass pans, a process which shaped a single sheet of brass into a hollow-ware vessel by beating, hence the term battery. The formation of a deep pan from a piece of brass was only achieved by several series of hammerings, each series followed by a complete annealing process. A large pan would go through the annealing ovens four or five times, before reaching the final hammering stage. Suitable sizes of small pans from 12in or so upwards were bound together in threes, inside one another, for several consecutive operations, with the outer pan, termed a ferrier, being turned in to hold them all together.[26]

The procedure (opposite) for shaping a pan from the flat circular sheet of brass called a nap (a) was as follows: the first blows radiated from the centre to the circumference whilst, at the same time, the nap was slowly revolved. This produced the initial curving of a pan, resulting in a cross-section similar to (b). After annealing, hammer blows deepened the curve, as at (c); with further annealing and hammering, as required, until the full depth had been obtained (d). Then, with the number of annealings dependent upon the size of pan being produced, the rim was turned over, as at (e).[27]

There are some indications that another type of hammer may also have been in use at the mills at one time.[28] This helve hammer, not to be confused with the helve shaft mentioned above, would have been of heavier construction, with the power transmitted from the shaft of the waterwheel by means of three or four cams lifting the hammer shaft at a point approaching the nose or head. This produced a much heavier, slower blow, with a far greater movement of the hammer head. Its purpose at Saltford and similar mills of the company would possibly have been to shape the large copper furnace-bottoms, known to have once been produced there. These

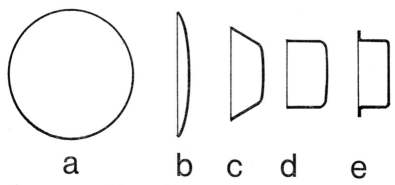

*Diagram of battery-pan production*

furnace-bottoms would not have required the dexterity of the light tilt hammer to beat out the large rounded base and the helve would therefore have been quite suitable, but no details of their use are documented and they have not functioned at Saltford within living memory.

The vessels produced by the tilt hammers were made from brass or copper sheet for both domestic and industrial purposes and, while special requirements could be satisfied, the main output consisted of the traditional types of hollow-ware vessels which the industry had always produced. At one period they were stamped with the trade-mark letters HBBCo. Neptunes were shallow dishes made up to 2ft 6in diameter with a depth of 3 to 6in, exported to the East for tea drying and to Africa for salt evaporation. Milk pans shaped like washing-up bowls were made up to 4ft diameter, particularly for the Welsh dairy trade, but the smaller sizes were called Lisbon pans, perhaps referring to the Bristol sugar industry which produced 'Lisbon' sugar. Kettles were deep straight-sided vessels with a handle but lacking a rim, made in various sizes.[29] In the eighteenth century they had been described as Guinea kettles and were produced for barter in Africa as part of the Bristol slave-trade system, but in later years the Harford company carefully avoided the full name. Nests of this type of vessel have been discovered on river bottoms of transport routes in North America—cargo lost en route to the early fur traders.[30] Small rounded bowls, with or without rims and handles, were known as cheffs or compass bowls, the latter possibly indicating their original purpose.

Guinea kettle              compass bowl

Lisbon pan                neptune pan

*Types of standard-production pans produced by the battery mills*
*not to scale*

The tilt hammers continued working until orders could no longer be obtained. The work ceased to be economic compared with the spun and pressed hollow-ware produced in the Midlands and, prior to the close of the nineteenth century, the men at Saltford were often short of work. At the turn of the century a large new order from Africa gave the mill a new lease of life, but the effect was only temporary. Saltford battery mill ground to a halt finally in 1908, the last of its kind to work brass in Great Britain, leaving only the Saltford rolling mill to continue working until 1925.

## The Brassworkers Themselves

The ancient equipment at the old mills required men who were willing to accept and master eighteenth-century methods of working. This was particularly so at the battery mills, where they sat on planks across the shallow pits containing the anvils of three hammers. Manipulating their brass vessels under the rapidly moving hammer heads, they were protected by leather knee-pads and aprons lined with very thin flexible brass sheet, and earplugs to guard against the intense noise. The last men to produce battery pans at the Saltford Mills in 1908 were Tom Shellard and George Brimble; the end of a long line of men who had carried on these traditional methods from the start of the old Bristol company more than 200 years before.[31]

Descendants of workers brought from the Low Countries were still employed at the brass mills in the very last stages. Old William 'Jarmin' Ollis was said to be of the ninth generation to work at Keynsham brass works, and descendants of his large family are still in business in Keynsham. Similar families represented as the industry came to a close, included the Frays and Frankhams. It was said that one branch of the Frankhams moved to Saltford mill when the lease of Kelston was relinquished, and census returns of 1851 lend support to this story.[32] The birth of John, 5 year old son of George Frankham, was recorded as taking place at Kelston Mills, but his sister, aged 2, was born at Saltford, thus giving a more accurate indication of the closure of Kelston Mills than is provided by other sources. Census returns also provide evidence of a branch of the Ollises moving from Kelston to Keynsham at a similar date, and undoubtedly many such families were moved as sites were closed down, one by one.

Henry Fray worked at Avon Mill in its final stages, the last representative of his family in the local industry. A few years before, in 1921, a local newspaper recalled the memories of his kinsman, Edwin Fray, then aged 88. He had started work at Avon Mill in 1842 at the age of 9, just after the construction of the Great Western Railway through the premises. He remembered this event well, particularly the pile-driving in the River Chew to enable the railway bridge to be built. He worked at the mill for sixty-six years.[33]

In his era, long hours were often worked by the men, and overtime was regarded as a privilege. 'We had good wages then', one old workman said. 'We were allowed to work as much overtime as we liked, and many a time I have worked nine days a week. I worked, Monday, Monday night and Tuesday and slept Tuesday night. Worked Wednesday, Wednesday night and Thursday, and slept Thursday night. Worked Friday, Friday night and Saturday, making nine days a week with good pay, I had handsfull of money to carry away on payday and hardly any time to spend it.' When asked what he did with the money, he replied, 'I drinked it, drinked it all, and had to lose time to do it'. He was then asked where he would have been if he had not spent the money in drink, and promptly replied, 'In my grave, Sir'. This should not, however, be taken as an indication of the general habits of the brassworkers. Many were teetotal, and pillars of the local nonconformist chapels.

Task work, this nine-day-week system, was frequently operated when a specified number of annealings or other processes made up a day's employment. It was even possible to work a greater number of days, and it is said that one man created a record by working thirteen days in one week, without having worked on a Sunday. He started in the early hours of Monday and finished late on Saturday night having taken his meals while at work and snatched some sleep between annealings to establish the record. He was then paid for his thirteen days' work. Some men slept at the mills, where iron bedsteads were provided for them, and it is interesting to note that some of these bedsteads were included in the catalogue for the 1862 auction (Appendix Two, page 229). It was possible to buy provisions from other workmen, and beer was sold at a penny per quart, with potatoes at 2s 6d per sack.

Some families lived on the premises, and children were born there who later worked at the mills all their lives. Several cash premiums and framed certificates were awarded by Bristol Agricultural Society to members of the firm for long service and good behaviour. The following are recorded in a newspaper account: £5 in 1838 to Mathias Johnson for 70 years' faithful servitude; £5 in 1841 to George Ollis for 60 years; £4 in 1844 to Robert Ford for 72 years; £4 in 1847 to Nicholas Ollis for 60 years; £4 in 1850 to George Lewis for 51 years; and £4 in 1854 to Jeremiah Deverill, for 54 years' service. The stated length of service does not necessarily show the full period of employment. It is known, for instance, that Jeremiah Deverill continued working for some years after his award, at least until 1859–60.[34]

In spite of the long span of employment in the industry covered by these men and their ancestors, few memories have been retained of the early formation of the company. The most persistent story handed down from the eighteenth century has been the Handel legend. According to any elderly brassworker, or indeed any old local family, the Hallelujah Chorus was written by Handel after he heard the incessant rhythm of the battery hammers at Keynsham, or at Saltford, according to the loyalties of the story-teller. It is worth noting that Handel's patron, the first Duke of Chandos, had family connections with the Bridges family of Keynsham, and it is not beyond the bounds of possibility that Handel could have accompanied the duke on a visit to Keynsham. In the parish church a brass offertory plate bears the rather crudely lettered inscription 'S John's Church Keynsham. G. F. Handel. 1750'. This is taken locally as strong evidence in support of the story; nevertheless, the industrial historian is more inclined to consider it as just one more version of a delightful legend that is found frequently in other parts of the country where water-powered hammers have been used.[35]

No memories remain of the society formed for the benefit of workers at the old Bristol company's Keynsham mills in 1780. In cases of sickness, 6s per week was to be paid, or 1s per day. Membership was limited to one hundred, and the organisation was named The Friendly Society of Workmen at the Brass Company's Works at Keynsham Mills. Unfortunately the agreement drawn up under this title can no longer be traced.[36]

As Bristol works declined rapidly and the Birmingham industry expanded, many local workers left the district to find employment in more prosperous areas. A. C. V. Davies, the last manager, knew of several Keynsham men working at Birmingham Battery & Metal Company; but many had left long before that era, as instanced by Joseph Harris who left Kingswood to manage a copper works for Thomas Williams at Liverpool in the late-eighteenth century. One of his descendants, Professor John R. Harris, still retains a link with the industry in his research into the history of the northern copper industries.[37] Charles Fray, a Keynsham brassworker, moved to the Birmingham area in 1854 and one of his descendants, George C. Fray, became the owner of a large manufacturing business concerned with fabricating copper-zinc alloys. George Fray himself found time to trace the lineage of his family from the workers brought from the Low Countries, as New Zealand descendants of the Craymer family have done more recently.[38] The Ollis family are still represented in the present-day industry by E. H. Ollis, a director of the Delta Metal Company.

In the final stages of the brass mills, the employees were no longer highly paid and no overtime or nightwork was available. Those who had cottages near the mills were expected to spend part of their nights, at certain times of the year, catching eels in

Page 175 (right) *This cogwheel can still be seen performing duty as a bollard outside the Old Brass Mill at Saltford. Wooden teeth were inserted in the slots which depressed the tail end of a battery hammer;* (below) *the only brass-battery hammer head still known to exist, height 12in*

Page 176 (above) *A finished brass-battery pan;* (below) *the engraving on the Handel Plate from Keynsham's parish church*

nets or 'hullies' set up at the mill hatches. For this they were paid half-a-crown per night, and the following day had to take their catches, varying from 4–15cwt, to be sold at Bath fishmongers.[39] The brass company, under the Bains and Davies', apparently found this extra income worthwhile.

Many workers took advantage of the privilege allowed them of buying metal at reduced rates and, by making it up in their own time, supplied their homes with domestic utensils and various kinds of ornament.[40] Many of these articles still survive in the Saltford and Keynsham homes of the workers and their descendants, but care should be taken not to confuse these cherished heirlooms with the commercial products of the mills. Both are reminders of the past industry where the work was hard and the equipment decrepit, but where men worked with pride and dignity in the traditional methods of Bristol brass.

L

# References

CHAPTER ONE: *A New Industry* (*pages 15–25*)

1 Hamilton, Henry. *The English Brass and Copper Industries to 1800* (1926, reprinted 1967), 15
2 Ibid, 1–16
3 Ibid, 14
4 Donald, M. B. *Elizabethan Monopolies* (1961), 13–23
5 Hamilton. *Brass and Copper Industries*, 13–15
6 Donald. *Elizabethan Monopolies*, 87–8
7 Ibid, 88–9
8 Rees, William. *Industry before the Industrial Revolution*, 2 (Cardiff, 1968), 392
9 Donald. *Elizabethan Monopolies*, 91–3
10 1cwt copper was first reported to yield 140lb then later 147lb brass, ie 75–69 per cent copper to 25–31 per cent zinc and impurities. See Alpha Brass in Glossary
11 Donald, *Elizabethan Monopolies*, 87, 91
12 Ibid, 187
13 Hamilton. *Brass and Copper Industries*, 19
14 Donald. *Elizabethan Monopolies*, 106–7, 181–3
15 Ibid, 189, 191–3; Gough, J. W. *The Mines of Mendip* (revised 1967, Newton Abbot), 211
16 Donald. *Elizabethan Monopolies*, 186–94
17 Hamilton. *Brass and Copper Industries*, 43–4, 58
18 British Museum. Loan 16, Court Books of the Society of Mineral & Battery Works, 3, 37–8
19 Ibid, 39–42; one noble equalled 6s 8d
20 Ibid, 44–6
21 Ibid, 53–7
22 Ibid, 57–60
23 Hamilton. *Brass and Copper Industries*, 59–60
24 Robey, John A. 'Ecton Copper Mines in the Seventeenth Century', *Bulletin Peak District Mines Historical Society*, 4, pt 2 (1969), 149–51; Hamilton. *Brass and Copper Industries*, 62
25 BM Loan 16, Court Books, 3, 132–3
26 Gough. *Mines of Mendip*, 214
27 BM Loan 16, Court Books, 3, 144–5
28 Gough. *Mines of Mendip*, 215
29 Hamilton. *Brass and Copper Industries*, 64

CHAPTER TWO: *Bristol Initiative (pages 26–47)*

1  Jenkins, Rhys. 'Copper Works at Redbrook and Bristol', *Transactions Bristol & Gloucestershire Archaeological Society*, 63 (1943), 145–54

2  Liverpool University Library, Rhys Jenkins Papers, translations of 'Thomas Cletscher's relations of European Mines in 1696', 13; and 'Eric Odelstierna's Travelling description over the foreign mines' (1691–3), 2

3  Gloucester Record Office, D1677 GG1352–7, 1709 Agreement

4  Houghton, John. *Husbandry and Trade Improv'd*, 3 (9 July 1697), 190, 192–4

5  *National Dictionary of Biography*, 5 (1964), 1044–5; Hamilton, Henry. *The English Brass and Copper Industries to 1800* (1926, reprinted 1967), 119

6  Glos RO, D1677 GG1352–7, 1709 Agreement

7  *Journal of the House of Commons* (1715), 178; Jenkins, Rhys. 'Copper Smelting in England: Revival at the end of the Seventeenth Century', *Transactions Newcomen Society*, 24 (1943–4), 74, 77

8  Raistrick, Arthur. 'The London Lead Company', *Transactions Newcomen Society*, 14 (1933–4), 119–26; Jenkins. 'Copper Works at Redbrook and Bristol', 162–3

9  Royal Institution of Cornwall Library, Tonkin MSS (Phillips MS 13495), 199 (17–18)

10  Science Museum Library, Rhys Jenkins Papers, Box 22, Exchequer Port Book extracts; LUL, Rhys Jenkins Papers, Cletscher, 7–15; Jenkins. 'Copper Works at Redbrook and Bristol', 163; RICL, 'The Farthest Answer of St John Aubyn to Gabriel Wayne'

11  LUL, Rhys Jenkins Papers, Cletscher, 7–17, 3–6

12  Jenkins. 'Copper Works at Redbrook and Bristol', 163–4

13  Raistrick, Arthur. *Dynasty of Ironfounders: The Darbys of Coalbrookdale* (1953, reprinted Newton Abbot 1970), 17–19

14  Mott, R. A. 'The Shropshire Iron Industry', *Transactions Shropshire Archaeological Society*, 56/1, 83; Houghton. *Husbandry and Trade Improv'd*, 1 (20 April 1693), 107

15  Raistrick. *Dynasty of Ironfounders*, 20–1

16  Public Record Office, Registers of Privy Council, 25 July 1700

17  *House of Commons Committee Reports*, 10 (1799), 666; Friends House Library, Norris MSS 10, Hannah Rose's 'Some Account of the Family of the Darbys', 122–5; Bristol Archives Office, Records of Society of Friends; British Museum, Add MSS 22675, f 36

18  FHL, Hannah Rose. 'Darbys', 134

19  *JHC* (1712), 160–3; Houghton. *Husbandry and Trade Improv'd*, 2 (1697), 184, 190; Galon, J. *L'Art de Convetir le Cuivre Rouge en Laiton ou Cuivre Jaune*, 1764; Swedenborg, Emanuel. *de Cupro* (1734), English translation, Searle, A. H., British Non-ferrous Metals Research Association, Misc Pub 333

20  Mott. 'Shropshire Iron Industry', 83

21  Houghton. *Husbandry and Trade Improv'd*, 2, 184; BM, Add MSS 22675;

Galon. *L'Art de Convetir le Cuivre Rouge en Laiton*, plate 19

22 *JHC* (1712), 161; Houghton. *Husbandry and Trade Improv'd,* 2, 184

23 Under the Julian Calendar in use until 1752, the old year ended on 24 March. In this period, dates between January and March have years converted to the new style in the text, ie this birth is recorded 25 January 1707 in the church registers

24 Latimer, John. *Annals of Bristol in the Eighteenth Century* (1893), 67

25 BM, Add MSS 22675, f 36. This legal document gives rather different information on the early partners of the company compared with the version accepted previously, by Hannah Rose, writing many years later; Bristol AO, Records of the Society of Friends; FHL, Hannah Rose. 'Darbys', 134

26 BM, Add MSS 22675, f 36

27 Bristol AO, Records of the Society of Friends, Digests of Registers

28 BM, Add MSS 22675, f 36

29 FHL, Hannah Rose. 'Darbys', 124–5

30 Mott, R. A. MS 'Revolution in Iron', 14, 189. I am indebted to Dr Mott for allowing me to read this chapter of his book, unpublished at the time of writing

31 Raistrick. *Dynasty of Ironfounders*, 21–6

32 Ibid, 23–39; Mott, R. A. 'Abraham Darby (I and II) and the Coal-Iron Industry', *Transactions Newcomen Society*, 31 (1967), 49–57

33 Mott. 'Revolution in Iron', 14, 192; Mott. 'Abraham Darby (I and II)', 61; Mott. 'Shropshire Iron Industry', 83; Mott. *The Triumphs of Coke* (1965), 16; Percy, John. *Metallurgy: Fuel; Fire-Clays; Copper; Zinc; Brass, etc* (1861), 612–17

34 *JHC* (1712), 161

35 Shrewsbury Record Office, Lord Brownlow Collection, 29 April 1710

36 Shrewsbury RO, Attingham Collection, 16 April 1713

37 BM, Add MSS 22675, v 36; Hamilton. *Brass and Copper Industries*, 149

38 BM, Add MSS 22675, v 36–f 37

39 Glos RO, D1628, Lloyd/Harford bundle, will of John Andrews, 1743

40 BM, 8223a 9 (53), *The Humble Petition of Abraham Elton, etc*

41 Ibid; *JHC* (1712), 161

42 Ibid; BM 8223e 9 (54), *The Case of the Manufacturers*

43 *JHC* (1711/12), 28, 132, 174; BM, 8245a 18, *A Brief Essay on the Copper and Brass Manufactures of England* (1712), 3–6

44 *JHC* (1712), 160–3

45 Ibid, 163

46 LUL, Rhys Jenkins Papers, translation of correspondence from Anders Swab to Bergskollegium: Foreign Mine Relations (1712), 2–3, 5

47 Jenkins. 'Copper Works at Redbrook and Bristol', 164; LUL, Rhys Jenkins Papers, translation of H. Kahlmeter's 'A relation of the English Mines in 1725', 45–6; LUL, Rhys Jenkins Papers, Anders Swab, 2–3, 5

48 Ibid, 2

49  BM, Add MSS 22675, f 37
50  Ibid, f 37–v 37
51  Dubois, Armand B. *The English Business Company after the Bubble Act 1720–1800* (New York, 1938), 30, 43 n12; Gower, L. C. B. *The Principles of Modern Company Law* (1957), 27–8
52  BM, Add MSS 22675, v 37
53  *JHC* (1721/2), 703–4
54  BM, 8245a 28, *The State of the Copper and Brass Manufactures in Great Britain* (1721), 1–9
55  *JHC* (1721/2), 719–20, 725, etc
56  *JHC* (1721/2), 734
57  BM, Add MSS 22675, f 75

CHAPTER THREE: *Early Techniques and Organisation* (*pages 48–72*)

1  Woolrich, A. P. 'Swedish Travellers', *BIAS Journal*, 4 (1971), 28–31; Liverpool University Library, Rhys Jenkins Papers, translation of H. Kahlmeter's 'A relation of the English Mines in 1725', 56
2  Chapter Two, 45
3  Public Record Office, C33/352, Cornish Mines Case, f 157–v 158; Royal Institution of Cornwall Library, 'The Farthest Answer of St John Aubyn to Gabriel Wayne'.
4  PRO, C33/352
5  LUL, Rhys Jenkins Papers, Kahlmeter, 3–6, 9, 28–33, 36–9
6  RICL, 'The Farthest Answer to Gabriel Wayne; Latimer, John. *Annals of Bristol in the Eighteenth Century* (1893), 66
7  RICL, Tonkin MSS (Phillips MS 13495), 18; Pryce, William. *Mineralogia Cornubiensis* (1778), 278; University College Swansea Library, Robert Morris MSS, 'A History of the Copper Concern', 21
8  Ibid, 9; National Library of Wales, MSS 15101–9
9  Science Museum Library, Rhys Jenkins Papers, Box 25, John Coster's will; LUL, Rhys Jenkins Papers, Kahlmeter, 8–9, 18, 24–5
10  Patent Specification No 397, 1714
11  Barton, D. B. *Copper Mining in Devon and Cornwall* (St Austell, 1961), 13
12  LUL, Rhys Jenkins Papers, Kahlmeter, 45, 64
13  Ibid, 46–60; Swedenborg, Emanuel. *de Cupro* (1734), English translation, Searle, A. H., British Non-ferrous Metals Research Association, Misc Pub 333. Kahlmeter and Swedenborg describe the same furnaces and processes, but a comparison reveals chronological errors in Swedenborg's account
14  LUL, Rhys Jenkins Papers, Kahlmeter, 45–61; Swedenborg. *de Cupro* (Searle), 342–3. The author is indebted to Dr Tylecote for his interpretation of the techniques in these sources
15  LUL, Rhys Jenkins Papers, Kahlmeter, 51, 61–2, 64–5

16 SML, Rhys Jenkins Papers, will of John Coster; Glamorgan Record Office, D/DXhr/12, Abstract of Title
17 Glam RO, D/DXhr/9; Somerset Record Office, DD/OB 103 (i)–105
18 Glam RO, D/DXhr/1, /19
19 UCSL, Robert Morris MSS, 'A History of the Copper Concern', 22; SML, Rhys Jenkins Papers, will of John Coster
20 Raistrick, Arthur. *Dynasty of Ironfounders: The Darbys of Coalbrookdale* (1953, reprinted Newton Abbot 1970), 10, 40
21 Rees, William. *Industry Before the Industrial Revolution*, 2 (Cardiff, 1968), 502; SML, Rhys Jenkins Papers, Box 22, Exchequer Port Book extracts
22 Specification of Patent No 454, 1723
23 LUL, Rhys Jenkins Papers, Kahlmeter, 65–7; Swedenborg. *de Cupro* (Searle), 342–3
24 Uppsala Universitetbibliotek, MS G130, Kahlmeter letters to Alströmer, 11 January 1724/5 (by courtesy of A. P. Woolrich).
25 LUL, Rhys Jenkins Papers, Kahlmeter, 65–7; Swedenborg. *de Cupro* (Searle), 342–3
26 Houghton, John. *Husbandry and Trade Improv'd*, 3 (13–20 August 1697), 203–6
27 Pooley, Giles. 'An Account of Digging and Preparing Lapis Calaminaris', *Philosophical Transactions* (1693), 673–6
28 Swedenborg. *de Cupro* (Searle), 335, 342
29 LUL, Rhys Jenkins Papers, Kahlmeter, 65, 68; Swedenborg. *de Cupro* (Searle), 342
30 Buck, N. and S. *Northwest Prospect of the City of Bristol* (1734)
31 Raistrick, Arthur (editor). *The Hatchett Diary* (Truro, 1967), 53–5
32 LUL, Rhys Jenkins Papers, Kahlmeter, 67–8; Swedenborg. *de Cupro* (Searle), 342–3
33 Houghton. *Husbandry and Trade Improv'd*, 3 (5 June 1696), 56; Webster, J. *Metallographia* (1671), 337–9
34 LUL, Rhys Jenkins Papers, Kahlmeter, 68; Swedenborg. *de Cupro* (Searle), 342–3
35 Ibid
36 Ibid
37 Hamilton, Henry. *The English Brass and Copper Industries to 1800* (1926, reprinted 1967), 148. Hamilton had access to several papers of the company which cannot now be traced. The Saltford deed is one of these
38 From details compiled by Mrs C. Turner
39 British Inland Waterways. Deeds of Weston, Bath, No 3341
40 Latimer. *Annals of Bristol, 18th Century*, 95
41 Boyce, Benjamin. *The Benevolent Man; A life of Ralph Allen of Bath* (New York, 1967), 110, 131; British Museum, Maproom K.XXXVIII.32.A 'A View of Twiverton near Bath'. Twiverton is an old spelling for Twerton, the parish on the south bank of the river

42 SML, Rhys Jenkins Papers, Box 16, Notes on Dr Pococke
43 Gloucester Record Office, D1628, Abstract of Leases on behalf of Edward Harford
44 Keynsham & Saltford Local History Society archives: Agreement between Parish of Keynsham and Brass Wire Work Company. In the previous century a similar agreement was made at Bradford-on-Avon, Wiltshire, concerning the local clothworkers
45 Indenture in possession of family of the late George C. Fray; K & SLHS archives, George C. Fray, 'The Keynsham Frays'
46 Bristol Reference Library, Ellacombe MSS 8, Donald Bain to Ellacombe, 26 June 1879
47 Som RO, DD/POT 69, Deeds of Woodborough Mill
48 Jenkins, Rhys. 'Copper Works at Redbrook and Bristol', *Transactions Bristol & Gloucestershire Archaeological Society*, 63 (1943), 155–6; Glam RO, D/DXhr1
49 Hamilton. *Brass and Copper Industries*, 146–7; Pryce. *Mineralogia Cornubiensis*, 287; UCSL, Robert Morris MSS, 'A History of the Copper Concern'
50 NLW, MSS 15101–9
51 Glos RO, D1677 GG1352–7
52 Glos RO, D1987/1
53 LUL, Rhys Jenkins Papers, translation of Reinhold Angerstein's 'Journal of the Journey through England in the Years 1753-4-5', 19–20
54 Bristol Archives Office, Minutes of Common Council, 18 August 1749
55 Rocque, J. *Plan of Bristol* (1742)
56 NLW, MSS 15101–9; UCSL, Morris MSS, 'A History of the Copper Concern', 9; LUL, Rhys Jenkins Papers, Angerstein, 17
57 Hamilton. *Brass and Copper Industries*, 156

CHAPTER FOUR: *William Champion and the Warmley Company (pages 73–94)*

1 *Journal of the House of Commons* (1750), 54
2 Watson, R. *Chemical Essays*, 4 (1786), 29–36
3 Cocks, E. J. and Walters, B. *A History of the Zinc Smelting Industry in Great Britain* (1968), 3–4 and illustration opp 7; Webster, J. *Metallographia* (1671), 337–9; Jenkins, Rhys. 'The Zinc Industry in England', *Transactions Newcomen Society* (1946), 42; Watson. *Chemical Essays*, 45–7
4 Ibid, 40–1; Beckmann, J. *History of Invention*, 2 (1797), 42
5 Jenkins. 'Zinc Industry', 42; University College Swansea Library, Robert Morris MSS, 'A History of the Copper Concern', 29
6 Neville Hall, Newcastle upon Tyne, Minute Books of London Lead Co, 5, 17 September 1723. Negotiation of mine leases in Tipperary with Dr Lane, Charles Harford and R. Champion. Information kindly made available to author by Dr J. N. Rhodes
7 Watson. *Chemical Essays*, 22–3; Jenkins. 'Zinc Industry', 46
8 *JHC* (1750), 54

9 Watson. *Chemical Essays*, 38–40
10 Mosselman, E. 'Fusion des Minerais de Zinc en Angleterre', *Annales des Mines* (1825), 486–90; Jenkins. 'Zinc Industry', 47 n
11 Percy, Joh. *Metallurgy: Fuel; Fire-Clays; Copper; Zinc; Brass, etc* (1861), 521
12 *JHC* (1750), 54; Bristol Archives Office, Minutes of Common Council, 4 September 1742 and 4 June 1743
13 *JHC* (1750), 54
14 British Museum, Add MSS 22675, f 75, Petition for Incorporation of Warmley Company; Gloucester Record Office, D421/B1 Bathurst Papers, W. Champion to R. Champion & BWCo, May 1761
15 National Library of Wales, MSS 15101–9
16 Ducarel, Dr. 'Method of Purifying Copper Ore and Making Brass', *Gentleman's Magazine*, 79, 821–2
17 *JHC* (1750), 54
18 Ibid, 81–2
19 *JHC* (1751), 150
20 *Bristol Journal*, 30 September 1749; Ellacombe, H. T. *History of the Parish of Bitton* (Exeter, 1883), 230
21 Raistrick, Arthur. *Dynasty of Ironfounders: The Darbys of Coalbrookdale* (1953, reprinted Newton Abbot 1970), 150
22 Hogshead equals 52½gal
23 Liverpool University Library, Rhys Jenkins Papers, translation of Reinhold Angerstein's 'Journal of the Journey through England in the Years 1753-4-5', 17–19
24 NLW, MSS 15101–9 (Appendix One, 214)
25 Ellacombe. *Bitton*, 229
26 Glos RO, D421/B1, endorsed 'an Acct of Warmley Co', 25 March 1761
27 Ellacombe. *Bitton*, 229
28 Glos RO, D421/B1, endorsed 'Mr Champion's First Proposals', 1761; Bristol AO, Records of Society of Friends, Digests of Registers
29 Bristol AO, MSS 24500 (3e), Abstract of Title, Baptist Mills, 1787; Rhodes, John N., PhD Thesis, and details of deeds communicated privately to author
30 Pennant, T. *History of Whitford and Holywell* (1796), 203
31 Glos RO, D421/B1, 'Champion's First Proposals'
32 Previously Wm Champion & Co. Often spelt Warmly in company papers, but not consistently, therefore the usual version has been used in text
33 Little, Bryan. 'Norbonne Berkeley: Gloucestershire Magnate', *Virginia Magazine of History & Biography* (USA, 1955), 63, 380–409; Glos RO, D421/B1, 'Champion's First Proposals'
34 Ibid, 'W. Champion to R. Champion & BWCo'
35 Ibid, 'Joseph Loscombe to Warmley Company', 4 June 1761
36 Jenkins, 'Zinc Industry', 48
37 Glos RO, D421/B1, 'Charles Bragge to Norbonne Berkeley', undated
38 Ibid, Charles Whittuck to (Charles Bragge?), 19 June 1761

39 Ibid, 7 July 1761 and 21 July 1761. The Horseshoe, a public house, still exists
40 Ibid, 'Champion's First Proposals'
41 Ibid, Charles Whittuck to Charles Bragge, 6 October 1761. One cart of coal equalled 1½ bushels
42 Glos RO, D421/B1, 'Present State and Constitution of Warmley Co, 25 March 1765
43 Ibid, 'Mr Champion's Plan for Carrying on Warmley Works'
44 Dubois, A. B. *The English Business Company after the Bubble Act* (New York, 1938), 30; Public Record Office, PC/1/737 Bristol Brass Co
45 Glos RO, D421/B1, 'State of Warmley Co's Stock, Debts and Effects', 1767
46 Russell, P. and Price, O. *England Displayed*, 1 (1769), 55
47 Glos RO, D421/B1, 'State of Warmley Co's Stock, Debts and Effects', 1767
48 Banks, Sir Joseph, 'Journal of an Excursion, May–June 1767', *Proceedings Bristol Naturalists Society*, 9/1 (1898). By courtesy of A. P. Woolrich
49 Donn, B. *Map of the Country 11 miles round the City of Bristol* (1769)
50 BM, Add MSS 22675, f 70, Petition for Incorporation
51 Glos RO, D421/B1, Bragge to Botetourt, 8 February 1767
52 Dubois. *English Business Company*, 30–40; BM Add MSS 22675, 70–80
53 Glos RO, D421/B1, Green to (Bragge?), 26 April 1768
54 Ibid, Bragge to Botetourt, 23 July 1768; Little. 'Norbonne Berkeley', 380–409
55 *Felix Farley's Bristol Journal*, 11 March 1769
56 Somerset House, will of Sampson Lloyd II, 2 January 1777. By courtesy of Humphrey H. Lloyd

CHAPTER FIVE: *The Decline of the Old Bristol Company (pages 95–116)*

1 British Museum, Add MSS 22675, f 74–5
2 Gloucester Record Office, D421/B1 Bathurst Papers, endorsed 'No 4, A Comparison between the BWCO and Warmley Co'
3 Pollard, Sydney. *The Genesis of Modern Management* (1955), 104; the Warmley Company was later said to be worth a much higher figure, but by then was widely mistrusted
4 Bristol Reference Library, MS B4771, the Committee Book of the Joseph Percival & Copper Co, 1762–9
5 Watson, R. 'Chemical Essays', 4 (1786), 83–4
6 Harris, J. R. 'The Copper Industry in Lancashire and North Wales', 2 (1952), Manchester PhD Thesis. The writer is indebted to Professor Harris, and to Dr John Robey, for information on the northern companies
7 Friends House Library, Lloyd MSS, Dolobran 89, Bristol Feb 1765, made available to the author by Humphrey H. Lloyd
8 Harris. 'The Copper Industry in Lancashire and North Wales'
9 Harris, J. R. *The Copper King* (Liverpool, 1964), 16–17

10 Chaloner, W. H. 'Charles Roe of Macclesfield, 1715–81', *Transactions Lancs & Cheshire Antiquarian Society*, 62 (1950–1); 63 (1952–3)

11 Rowlands, John. *Copper Mountain* (Llangefni, 1966), 1–26; Harris. *Copper King*, 18–35

12 Chaloner. 'Charles Roe of Macclesfield', 62, 55–65; Harris. *Copper King*, 163

13 University College of North Wales Library, Mona Mine MSS 3028–32

14 Chaloner. 'Charles Roe of Macclesfield', 62, 58

15 Harris. *Copper King*, 36–40

16 *Aris's Birmingham Gazette*, 9 October 1780

17 Hamilton, Henry. *The English Brass and Copper Industries to 1800* (1926, reprinted 1967), 134–9

18 Liverpool University Library, Rhys Jenkins Papers, translation of Reinhold Angerstein's 'Journal of the Journey through England in the Years 1753-4-5', 1–2

19 Aitken, W. C. 'Brass and Brass Manufactures', *Birmingham and the Midland Hardware District*, edited Timmins (1866, reprinted 1967), 237

20 Watson. *Chemical Essays*, 81–2

21 Hamilton. 'Brass and Copper Industries', 214–16

22 Ibid, 346–7. The stamping process was introduced to Birmingham by Richard Ford, who patented a method in 1769, No 935, shortly after John Pickering of London had obtained a patent for limited application of the process with No 920, 1769; *House of Commons Committee Reports*, 10 (1799), 660, 675

23 Hutton, W. *An History of Birmingham* (1795), 114

24 Aitken, 'Brass and Brass Manufactures', 243–4

25 Harris. *Copper King*, 16

26 *Aris's Birmingham Gazette*, 9 October 1780

27 Ibid, 16 October 1780

28 Birmingham Assay Office, Boulton Papers, C1/84/86

29 Ibid, C1/86

30 Hamilton. *Brass and Copper Industries*, 214–16

31 Birmingham AO, Boulton Papers, C1/84–100

32 Ibid, C1/91–3

33 Ibid, W1/112

34 Ibid, C1/100

35 Ibid, C1/84–100 and W1/112

36 Hamilton. *Brass and Copper Industries*, 119–24; Harris. *Copper King*, 41

37 Ibid, 40–53

38 Ibid, 54–68

39 Ibid, 70–80; Harris, J. R. and Roberts, R. O. 'Eighteenth Century Monopoly: The Cornish Metal Company Agreements of 1785', *Business History*, 5, 80–1

40 Hamilton. *Brass and Copper Industries*, 230

41 *Bristol Gazette & Public Advertiser*, 4 May 1786

42 Bristol Archives Office, 24500(3)e f 9, Baptist Mills Deeds; Records of Society of Friends, Digest of Registers

43  *Sarah Farley's Bristol Journal*, 23 December 1786 to 24 February 1787
44  Ibid, 3 March 1787
45  Bristol AO, 24500(3)e; Glos RO, D1628, Abstract of Articles of Copartnership, 31 March 1788
46  Harris. *Copper King*, 80–100
47  Roberts, R. O. 'The Copper Industry of Neath and Swansea', *South Wales & Monmouth Record Society*, 4 (1957), 125–36; National Library of Wales, MS 15112c (written 1811, referring to events about twenty years earlier)
48  Birmingham AO, Boulton Papers, C1/97
49  Jars, Gabriel. *Voyages Métallurgiques* (Lyons, 1774), 222–3
50  Harris. *Copper King*, 100–38; Hamilton. *Brass and Copper Industries*, 231–6
51  *House of Commons Committee Reports*, 10 (1799), 666
52  Cave, Sir Charles. *A History of Banking in Bristol* (Bristol, 1899), 90–9, 109; Harford, Alice. *Annals of the Harford Family* (1909), 33, 38
53  Minute Book of the Cheadle Brass Wire Company, transcribed by Dr John Robey, 'now an extreme depression in Trade . . . owing to the number of persons in Birmingham manufacturing wire', 7 September 1819
54  Rudder, Samuel. *A New History of Gloucestershire* (1779), 663; Birmingham Reference Library, Boulton & Watt Papers, Box 2H, April 1784; Ellacombe, H.T. *History of the Parish of Bitton* (Exeter, 1883), 230
55  Glos RO, Land Tax Records; D1987, Deeds of Conham Estate
56  NLW, Lord Swansea Collection, Accounts of Copper Sold. Ticketings of sales to Harfords & Brass Wire Company cease at 1818
57  Deeds of Conveyance Crew's Hole, transcription made by Ewart Lovell and kindly shown to the author; Deeds of Warmley House seen by arrangement with Warmley UDC
58  Somerset Record Office, DD/PO18, Court Rolls of Compton Dando Manor, 1791 references to the brass mills being ruinous
59  Glos RO, Land Tax Records for Bitton; Somerset RO, Land Tax Records for Weston, Bath
60  Latimer, John. *Annals of Bristol in the Eighteenth Century* (1893), 50; Glos RO, D1628, Messrs Sturge's Report, 1830
61  *Bristol Mirror*, 18 June 1831
62  Bristol AO, 24500(3), Deeds of Baptist Mills; Glos RO, D1628, Messrs Sturge's report on property at Keynsham and Saltford, 17 February 1855

CHAPTER SIX: *Later Bristol Developments (pages 117–43)*

1  *Aris's Birmingham Gazette*, 9 October 1780
2  Bristol Archives Office, Records of Society of Friends, Digests of Registers; National Library of Wales, Powis MSS 3840, 3353, 3564; Wynnstay MSS, Box X, No 31, etc
3  Friends House Library, Lloyd Papers, Rachel Barclay to Nehemiah Lloyd, 19 July 1774. By courtesy of Humphrey H. Lloyd

4 University College of North Wales Library, Mona Mine MSS 3028–32, 3544 f 13
5 Bristol AO, Friends' Digest of Registers
6 UCNWL, Mona Mine MSS 3544
7 Birmingham Assay Office, Boulton Papers, C1/100, Thos Williams, 2 and C2/39–40
8 Bristol AO, Friends' Digests of Registers
9 Ellacombe, H. T. *History of the Parish of Bitton* (Exeter, 1883), 228
10 *Aris's Birmingham Gazette*, 9 October 1780
11 Watson, R. *Chemical Essays*, 4 (1786), 45–7
12 Birmingham AO, Boulton Papers, C1/97, Capper to Boulton
13 Watson. *Chemical Essays*, 9, 50
14 Birmingham AO, Boulton Papers, C1/107
15 Patent Specification No 1297, 31 October 1781
16 Watson. *Chemical Essays*, 45–8
17 *Felix Farley's Bristol Journal*, 19 March 1803
18 Ibid, 18 June 1803
19 Hanham Ratebooks, from extracts compiled by Ewart Lovell
20 Gloucester Record Office, Land Tax Records for Barton Regis, 1780–4
21 Cave, Sir Charles. *A History of Banking in Bristol* (Bristol, 1899), 50–2
22 Macclesfield Company Minute Book, from extracts compiled by Professor J. R. Harris, and made available to the author
23 Muspratt, Sheridan. *Chemistry: The Art and Manufactures*, 1 (1854), 524
24 Glos RO, Land Tax Records for Barton Regis, etc, 1780–1800; Somerset Record Office, DD/PO 73, Popham Deeds
25 Birmingham AO, Boulton Papers, W1/121
26 Pryce, George. *History of Bristol* (Bristol, 1861), 220–3; Latimer, John. *Annals of Bristol in the Eighteenth Century* (1893), 438
27 Birmingham Reference Library, Boulton & Watt Papers, Box 6c, John Champion to Charles Lloyd, 15 July 1790
28 Ibid, James Watt to John Champion, 26 July 1790; John Champion to Boulton & Watt, 15 November 1793 and 19 December 1793
29 Patent Specification No 2239, 18 June 1798
30 *Felix Farley's Bristol Journal*, 1 December 1798
31 Ribblesdale Family Muniments, MM 111–19, transcribed by Dr Arthur Raistrick and kindly shown to the author
32 *Victoria County History: Gloucestershire*, 10 (1972), 150
33 Macclesfield Company Minute Book
34 *Bristol Gazette & Public Advertiser*, 11 January 1781
35 Birmingham AO, Boulton Papers, P2/236, T. Pike to Boulton, 10 June 1786
36 Glos RO, D182v/28
37 *Bristol Gazette*, 17 August 1809
38 *Bristol Directories*

39 Houghton, John. *Husbandry and Trade Improv'd*, 3 (13–20 August 1697), 203–6

40 Latimer. *Annals of Bristol in the Eighteenth Century*, 453–4; Cave. *Banking in Bristol*, 159, 238

41 Patent Specification No 2842, 29 April 1805. Working temperature was specified as between 210° to 300° F

42 Patent Specification No 4773, 8 April 1823. Working temperature was specified as about the heat of boiling water

43 Opinion of Dr R. F. Tylecote

44 Public Record Office, Court of Bankruptcy 1832/3 B4 (Ind 22678) January 32–July 34

45 *Bristol Gazette*, 24 May 1832

46 *Bristol Directories*, 1832–45

47 *Bristol Mirror*, 27 October 1838

48 Ralph, E. 'Notes on the Capper Pass Family', *Newsletter Gloucester Society for Industrial Archaeology*, 4 (1965), 13

49 Warren, Kenneth. *The British Iron and Steel Sheet Industry* (1970), 34–5; Cocks, E. J. and Walters, B. *A History of the Zinc Smelting Industry* (1968), 32–42

50 Glos RO, D1628; Keynsham UDC Offices, Ratebooks, 1834–5

51 *Bristol Mirror*, 13 June 1835

52 Glos RO, D1628, Sturge Report 1839; Aitken, W. C. 'Brass and Brass Manufacture', *Birmingham and the Midland Hardware District*, edited Timmins (1866, reprinted 1967), 236

53 Hunt, Robert. *British Mining* (1887), 905

54 Glos RO, D1628, Valuation of Property, Sturge 1830; William Armstrong to Messrs Harfords & BBCo, 10 June 1841; valuation by J. P. Sturge, 17 February 1855

55 NLW, Lord Swansea Collection, Walker to Vivian, 17 June 1828. Vivian was producing Best Copper for Harfords & BBCo

56 Glos RO, D1628, Edmund Lloyd to J. P. Sturge, 13 February 1855; Estate of S.Ll. Harford, 30 January 1854

57 Ibid, Sturge Valuations, 17 February, 5 March 1855; Particulars and Conditions of Sale, 7 July 1859

58 *Bristol Mirror*, 25 December 1858; Glamorgan Record Office, D/DXhr

59 *Bristol Mirror*, 25 January 1862; Glos RO, D1628, Osborne Ward & Co to Harfords & Brass Works, 3 January 1862; J. W. Miles to Harfords & BBCo, 15 July 1862

60 Keynsham UDC Offices, Deeds of Chew Mill

61 Bristol Reference Library, Ellacombe MSS 8, 48; for details of the specialised use of shoe rivets in the Kingswood industry, see Braine, A. *A History of Kingswood Forest* (1891, reprinted Bath 1968), 243

62 Messrs E. S. & A. Robinson, Deeds of Avon Mill, Bundle 1/10, Agreement 13 February 1902

63 Ibid, Schedule of Deeds

CHAPTER SEVEN: *The Old Mills: Work and Workers (pages 144–77)*

1  Aitken, W. C. 'Brass and Brass Manufacture', *Birmingham and the Midland Hardware District*, edited Timmins (1866, reprinted 1967), 236

2  Latimer, John. *Annals of Bristol in the Eighteenth Century* (1893), 67

3  Gloucester Record Office, D1628, Sturge Report 1839; Davies, A. C. V. (last manager of Harfords & Bristol Brass Company), correspondence with George Watkins, c 1941. Transcriptions and notes kindly made available to author

4  Ellacombe, H. T. *History of the Parish of Bitton* (Exeter, 1883), 230; deeds of Warmley House, seen by arrangement with Warmley UDC

5  Shellard, T. G. (ex-employee of H & BBCo), conversation with the author; Davies to Watkins correspondence

6  Gane, Miss E. (daughter of Charles Gane, late employee of H & BBCo), conversation with the author

7  Gowland, W. *The Metallurgy of Non-Ferrous Metals* (1921), 60; Dennis, W. H. *Metallurgy of the Non-Ferrous Metals* (1961), 176; Copper Development Association, *Brasses and other Copper-Zinc Alloys* (1935, revised 1956), 1–5

8  Davies to Watkins correspondence

9  Shellard, A. E. (ex-employee of H & BBCo), conversation with author; Shellard, T. G. to author; Davies to Watkins correspondence

10  Aitken, 'Brass and Brass Manufacture', 225

11  Copper Development Association, *Brass Pressings* (1937), 43–4

12  Davies to Watkins correspondence; Shellard, T. G. and Shellard A. E. to author

13  Specifications of Patents No 454, 1723; No 867, 1767

14  Shellard, T. G. to author

15  Davies to Watkins correspondence

16  Ibid

17  Glos RO, D1628, Sales Catalogue 1862

18  Shellard, T. G. to author

19  Davies to Watkins correspondence

20  Shellard, T. G. and Shellard, A. E. to author

21  Barnett, Harry (ex-employee of H & BBCo), conversation with author; Shellard, T. G. to author; Davies to Watkins correspondence

22  Ibid; Shellard, T. G. to author

23  Glos RO, D1628, Sturge Valuations 1830, 1839, 1855; Sales Catalogue 1862

24  de Soyres, B. 'History and Particulars of the Brass Battery Process', *Transactions Newcomen Society*, 28 (1952), 131–5; Davies to Watkins correspondence; Shellard, T. G. to author

25  Ibid. In July 1972, a complete cast-iron cogwheel 4ft diameter was exposed in a sewage trench in the road outside Saltford Mill. It was left in place and a small portion can still be seen acting as a protective bollard for the road-side wall (see plate on page 175)

26 Davies, A. C. V. 'Description of the Harford and Bristol Brass Company Methods of Making Battery', *The Birmingham Battery and Metal Company— One Hundred Years* (1936) 37–8; Shellard, T. G. to author

27 Shellard, T. R. (one of the last battery workers), conversation with George Watkins, c 1941

28 Shellard, T. G. to author, quoting memories of elderly workers he had known in his youth; Barnett to author

29 Bristol Reference Library, Ellacombe MSS 8, 48, Donald Bain to Ellacombe, 2 July 1879; Davies. 'Description of H & BBCo Methods'

30 Bass, George F. *Archaeology under Water* (1966), 40–3; 'Divers Discover 175 Year Old Kettles on Trade Route', *Minnesota Historical Society Newsletter* (1962); correspondence with Kenneth Kidd, Ontario

31 Shellard, T. G. to author; de Soyres. 'Brass Battery Process', 135

32 Public Record Office, Census Returns 1851, Saltford

33 *Western Daily Press*, 15 April 1921

34 Ibid, 5 May 1927

35 de Soyres. 'Brass Battery Process', 132; Fairclough, Mary. *History of the Parish Church of St John the Baptist, Keynsham*

36 Hamilton, Henry. *The English Brass and Copper Industries to 1800* (1926, reprinted 1967), 325, 370

37 Harris, J. R. *The Copper King* (Liverpool, 1964), 38–9 n

38 Keynsham & Saltford Local History Society Archives, George C. Fray. 'The Keynsham Frays'; Harry and Constance Craymer. 'Craymer Family Tree'

39 Shellard, T. G. to author

40 Ibid

# Glossary

SOME terms have been taken from tape-recordings of conversations with Keynsham or Saltford brassworkers. Of those words listed as local, some may have been used only in the area; others in more general use appear to have been connected with terms brought by early immigrant workers.

ALLOY. A metallic substance consisting of a mixture of two or more elements. Brass is a copper-zinc alloy.

ALPHA BRASS. A modern term denoting brass with a particular crystalline structure. A content of 20–37 per cent zinc, alloyed with 80–63 per cent copper, produced alpha brass, which is characterised by strength and considerable ductility when worked cold into sheet, batteryware and wire. These were processes in which the brass mills in Bristol specialised, and it is possible that they only produced brasses within this range, although the term would have been unknown to them.

ANNEALING. Heat treatment to soften work-hardened metal. Without this treatment, further manipulation of work-hardened brass can cause the metal to crack. Correct temperatures and periods of heating are necessary, but men at the works in the Bristol area relied on their own judgement of the appearance of the metal in the furnaces.

ANNEALING OVEN. A furnace in which the annealing process was carried out was usually described as an oven, both by the men and in documentary sources. The modern metallurgist would prefer to call it a furnace.

BATTERY or BATTERYWARE. Metal which has been extended and shaped by beating with a hammer. Originally denoted sheet metal of iron, brass or copper, but by the eighteenth century came to be employed more specifically for hollow-ware vessels of brass and copper.

BIRMINGHAM SINGLE-POT FURNACE. Furnace designed to take a single crucible for the direct method of brass melting. Believed by the Keynsham workers to have been developed in Birmingham.

BLACK BATTERY. Battery which has not received the final pickling or brightening process.

BLACK JACK. Zinc Sulphide (ZnS), otherwise known as blende. An ore of zinc which, according to Patent No 726, was first used by John Champion in 1758. Now known as sphalerite, and the main source of zinc, it is used in large quantities at the zinc-smelting works at Avonmouth. In the Bristol area the term is sometimes used mistakenly to refer to the copper-slag blocks employed as a building material.

BLACK LATTEN or LATTIN. Brass sheet or partially shaped sheet which has not received the final pickling or brightening process. *See* LATTEN.

BLENDE. *See* BLACK JACK.

BLOCK. A die with a graduated series of tapered holes, used for drawing wire; also known generally in the industry as a wortle or wortle plate. The term was also used at Keynsham to describe a complete set of equipment on a wiredrawer's bench.

BOSH. A large brass bowl or trough, kept filled with water at the door of each annealing furnace. A blacksmiths' term.

BOTTOMS. *See* COPPER BOTTOMS.

BRASS. A general term for the range of alloys produced from varying proportions of zinc and copper, although sometimes confined to those within the range of 60–80 per cent copper to 40–20 per cent zinc. Alloys with less than 20 per cent zinc to copper are nowadays referred to as gilding metals, but in the eighteenth century were known by such names as Mannheim gold, Prince's metal, pinchbeck or tomback. Brasses containing greater percentages of zinc than 37 per cent, were produced increasingly from the early nineteenth century, being more suited to hot-working processes. It is

M

unlikely that the Bristol industry was involved to any extent with the alloys at either end of the range. *See* ALPHA BRASS.

BREAKING DOWN. The initial stages of rolling a slab of brass into metal sheet.

BRISTOL BRASS. Bristol brass is sometimes listed as a specific grade of the metal in early nineteenth-century reference works on technical subjects (*Tomlinson's Cyclopaedia*, etc). The descriptions vary, but all are probably referring to a brass which would be described today as 70 per cent copper to 30 per cent zinc, or something near this.

BUCKLE or BUCK HOLE. The ashpit under the fire of an annealing furnace. Local.

BUDDLE. Trough, usually circular, used for concentrating pulverised ore in water.

CALAMINE. Zinc carbonate ($ZnCO_3$), an ore of zinc found on Mendip and other carboniferous-limestone regions of Great Britain. Used for the production of brass until after the mid-nineteenth century; at Keynsham only until the 1830s. Prior to the eighteenth century, calamine was commonly thought to be a non-metallic earthy substance, which merely changed the colour and weight of copper. The name calamine is also applied commercially nowadays to zinc silicate ($ZnSiO_4H_2O$) which does not enter into the history of the Bristol brass industry. Further confusion has been caused by the fact that in the USA, zinc carbonate ($ZnCO_3$), the calamine of Mendip, is known as Smithsonite.

CALAMINE BRASS. Brass made by smelting calcined calamine with broken or granulated copper in the presence of charcoal, or sometimes powdered coal. Only the briefest description of the Bristol method of making calamine brass has been discovered. A general idea of the current technique at about the time it was abandoned at Baptist Mills is given in *Rees's Manufacturing Industry* (*1819–20*), I (Newton Abbot, 1973), 221, 222, believed to have been written around 1805. A later and more scientific description of the process may be found in Percy's *Metallurgy*, 4 (1861), 612–18; but it is not contemporary with Bristol practice.

CALAMY. An eighteenth-century word for calamine.

CALCINATION. The application of heat to an ore, or partially pre-pared metalliferous material, to alter its physical structure and/or expel a part of the material, eg water. Calcination decomposed calamine ($ZnCO_3$) to zinc oxide ($ZnO$), suitable for the brass-making process, by expelling carbon dioxide ($CO_2$) to the atmos-phere. This was usually carried out near the mine to reduce the weight of the ore and thus lessen transport costs.

CASING. Very thin brass sheet produced at Saltford, and possibly other local mills, prior to the twentieth century. Mainly used in the Midlands industry for covering, or casing, ironware.

CAST. The particular way in which wire was wound on a reel. Keynsham wire was reputed to have a special cast which defied all attempts at copying. It is not known how this was achieved.

CEMENTATION. The method of making calamine brass was described as cementation. There were some similarities with the process of making cementation steel by the diffusion of carbon into wrought iron, without melting it, inside the cementation furnace. Zinc oxide diffused into unmelted copper inside the brass furnace.

CHEFF. A small shallow brass bowl, with a handle made usually from a cylinder of brass, but it could be of wood. Sometimes called a compass bowl, particularly if without a handle, and perhaps this denoted the original purpose of this shape of hollow-ware. Local.

CINDER. Furnace slag. Used to describe copper slag deposited on the bank of the Avon in the early eighteenth century.

COGS. In the battery mill, these were removable wooden teeth, wedged in apertures of the wooden or cast-iron cog ring which was fixed on an extension of the shaft of the waterwheel. They could be placed variably according to the speed required at the hammer head. Each revolving cog depressed the tail end of the hammer shaft, or helve, just a few inches, and thus the modern engineer would perhaps prefer to call them cams or tappets, but the men in the battery mills always referred to cogs.

COGWHEEL. In the battery mill this term referred to the ring carrying the inserted wooden cogs by which the hammers were depressed.

COMPASS BOWL. *See* CHEFF.

COPPER BOTTOMS. The bases of large industrial hollow-ware vessels, such as furnaces, stills and vats, appear to have been prepared in the battery mills to standard measurements, and were then often sold to other manufacturers who made up individual items to special requirements. The Bristol brass-battery mills are believed to have made these, but the copper mills of Coster/Joseph Percival/John Freeman Company appear to have particularly specialised in them.

CUPOLA or CUPILO or CUPELA. A reverberatory furnace used in Bristol and other early copper and lead-smelting areas during the late seventeenth and eighteenth centuries. The term was also used for the complete premises containing several such furnaces. The names still survive on maps of the mid-nineteenth century in the Bristol area. Believed to have been derived from the earliest furnaces of this type which had domed roofs (see Rhys Jenkins, 'Early Reverberatory Furnaces', *Transactions, Newcomen Society*, 19). The iron-melting cupola uses a quite different principle and is not in any way connected with this interpretation.

CURL. Length of strip brass wound into a roll for insertion into an annealing furnace. Local.

DILLEY. A long-handled trolley used for transporting heavy goods round the mill premises (plate, page 122). Local.

DIRECT METHOD. The method of making brass by melting metallic zinc with copper. Patented by James Emerson of Hanham, Bristol, in 1781, it eventually replaced the old cementation method using calcined calamine.

DUCTILITY. The property which enables a metal to be deformed without fracturing, an essential requirement for wiredrawing, as well as other processes not carried out in the Bristol area. Keynsham brass was reputed to be extremely ductile. *See* MALLEABILITY.

FERRIER. The outer pan of a number, often three, which were

placed one inside the other, when suitably sized, to be shaped up under the battery hammers. Local.

FINISHING. The final rolling stages in the preparation of brass sheet, for which a special pair of rolls was used.

FIRE. A full load for an annealing furnace. Local.

FLOAT. Paddle of a waterwheel.

FLUX. Material added during a smelting process to enable substances to be eliminated by combining with it and forming slag. The slag then floats on the top of the liquid metal, and can thus be separated by tapping. Fluxes are chosen for their natural affinity with the impurity being eliminated. Several different fluxes were employed in various stages of copper-smelting.

GRAPHITE. *See* PLUMBAGO.

GUINEA KETTLE. A kettle or straight-sided pan, made in large numbers during the eighteenth century for export to the Guinea or African coast. A product used for barter in slave-trading carried out from the Port of Bristol.

HELVE. The shaft of a battery hammer, either a tilt or helve hammer, and made of beechwood in the battery mills of the Bristol area.

HELVE HAMMER. A type of powered hammer, most commonly used in the iron industry, which may have been employed in the early brass-battery mills of the Bristol area. In contrast to the more usual tilt hammers which were depressed at the tail end, the helve hammer was lifted at the nose end, or else part-way along the shaft or helve, whilst being pivoted from the tail. The lift was usually given by three or four large cams on a revolving drum, which gave a slower, heavier blow suitable for heavier and less intricate work than the usual brass-battery production. However, memories of old workmen appear to suggest that it was formerly used for preparing bottoms of large hollow-ware vessels. *See* COPPER BOTTOMS.

HUSK or HURSK. A heavy oval cast-iron ring encircling the shaft of a battery hammer. It was fitted with two trunnions which nested in brass cups inserted in the heavy wooden posts either side of the hammer-shaft, allowing the hammer to pivot (page 166). Local.

JACOBITE. A pair of pincers which gripped the end of wire in the setting-up operation of wiredrawing at Keynsham. Local.

KETTLE. A straight-sided pan without a rim, usually with a handle.

KILLOT. A three-legged stand to hold trays of wire in the annealing furnace. Local.

KILN. The calcining kilns used in certain processes of eighteenth-century copper smelting would today be called furnaces. The relevant documentary sources, however, refer to kilns, and this is the term which has been used in the text.

LAPIS CALAMINARIS. The old scholars' name for calamine, still in use in the eighteenth century (see Watson's *Chemistry*, 4, 1786).

LATTEN or LATTIN. An old word for brass, believed to have been derived from the French *laiton*, which came to be more commonly used for brass sheet. Employed thus at Saltford and Keynsham until the works closed.

LIBERTY. Area owned by a Lord of the Mines in Bristol coalmining district.

LISBON PAN. A fairly shallow brass pan with a rim, produced in the Bristol area. The name has been attributed to the crystallised-fruit industry of Portugal, to where the pans were said to have been exported; but is more likely to have been derived from the Bristol sugar industry, which produced the 'whitest clayed' or 'Lisbon' sugars (see Robin Stiles, 'The Old Market Sugar Refinery', *BIAS Journal*, 2, 10).

MALLEABILITY. The property which enables a metal to be spread by hammering, without cracking. As this operation was carried out frequently at the Bristol brass mills, the grade of brass used had to be malleable. *See* DUCTILITY.

MANILLA. A crescent-shaped ingot of copper used as currency in Africa during the eighteenth century. Produced at Bristol for this trade.

MATTE. The impure metalliferous material produced when smelting sulphide ores of certain metals. Copper is gradually concentrated in a matte during successive operations of smelting copper sulphide ores.

MELTING. The modern brassmaking process making use of metallic zinc and copper is described as melting, as no chemical change takes place in the materials used. The older method using calamine and copper involved a smelting operation. *See* SMELTING.

METAL-PREPARED. Partially prepared brassware. Ingots of brass were so described prior to the eighteenth century, but afterwards the term came to mean unfinished hollow-ware vessels. By being so described, brassware was able to escape a large proportion of custom duty when imported into England during the eighteenth century.

MIXER. The man responsible for the calculations in making the different qualities of brass at Keynsham. This could be quite a complicated procedure when various grades of scrap metal were being used. Local.

MOULD. An ingot of brass, of a flat rectangular shape produced for rolling into sheet, or long and thin for preparing wire. The term is also used, more conventionally, for the shape into which the metal was cast.

MUFFLE FURNACE. A furnace with heating cavities surrounding, but separate from, the interior.

NAP. Brass sheet cut to a roughly circular shape, for hammering into a hollow-ware vessel. Local.

NEALING. Commonly used by the men, and in documentary sources. *See* ANNEALING.

NEGRO. A length of copper rod intended to be wound round the arm or leg for decorative purposes. Produced for the African market.

NEPTUNE. Thin shallow pan made for export to Africa where it is believed to have been used for salt making.

PLATES. Large flat rectangular slabs of metal, cast between granite moulds for subsequently hammering down to sheet metal.

PLUMBAGO. Graphite or blacklead. A carbon material which neither melts nor softens in furnaces, and so often used for crucibles. Plumbago crucibles replaced those made of clay for the brass-melting process in the latter years at Keynsham.

POTLINK. The linking mechanism connecting the drive from the waterwheel to the jacobite, the reciprocating pincers used for setting up the wiredrawing process at Avon Mill, Keynsham. Local.

PRITCHEL. A pointed tool, used for marking metal to pattern or size.

RAISE. To extend metal by hammering, particularly to shape a vessel.

REDUCTION. A process of smelting during which oxygen is removed from a compound.

REVERBERATORY FURNACE. A horizontal furnace in two sections. Draught created at one end by the chimney draws the furnace gases from the firegrate at the opposite end. From here, they are drawn over a low barrier into the main chamber, to follow the curved line of the roof. There the heat is reflected, or reverberated, down on to the charge in the furnace, and the gases then enter a duct to the chimney. Copper was smelted in early furnaces of this type in works at Conham, Crew's Hole, Warmley, etc, where they were described as cupolas.

RINGS. Components of a waterwheel. The two circular frames at the circumference of the wheel, on which the paddles or floats are mounted.

ROASTING. The process of heating metalliferous materials to temperatures short of their melting points, in order to effect chemical changes.

ROLLING MILL. Machinery for rolling, or extending, metal. Brass-rolling mills in the Bristol area were two-high, ie with two rolls, mounted one above the other. They were powered by water, usually with only the bottom roll driven. In the cases where both rolls were driven, separate waterwheels were used for each roll.

RUMPLE. Wire, drawn in the first operation of the wiremaking process, when it still resembles a thin rod. Local.

RUMPLE PRITCHEL. A sizing tool for re-opening the hole of a block, or wortle plate, to its correct diameter for drawing wire of a particular gauge. Local.

SHAB. An impurity of brass appearing on the surface of the metal, which had to be removed before the work could be given the finishing process, particularly when rolling sheet. It could be caused by scale, or improperly mixed metal, or foreign matter. It was usually removed with a pritchel. Local.

SHRUFF. Scrap brass. Offcuts of sheet after they have been cut to size, waste wire, etc. An essential ingredient of many methods of brassmaking. At the Bristol mills it was carefully saved and returned to the melting house for re-use. The term was derived from continental sources and there are slightly different derivations in the pottery, and iron and steel, industries.

SHUFF. Shruff. The version commonly used by men at Saltford and Keynsham. Local.

SLAB. A flat rectangular ingot of brass, produced for rolling into sheet. Local.

SLIP. A long narrow ingot of brass, produced for wire preparation. The same term was also used for strip in various stages of production. Local.

SLIP ROLLS. A pair of narrow rolls, used for preparing brass strip and slip intended for wire production. Local.

SLITTING MILL. Equipment used for cutting brass sheet or strip into narrow strips. This consisted of two revolving spindles, mounted one above the other, carrying circular cutting-discs which could be adjusted by spacing collars to set the top set to meet with the bottom, so forming several pairs of revolving shears.

SMELTING. The process in the production of metals where chemical changes occur in a molten furnace charge.

SPELTER. Zinc metal in its commercial form. Used from the seventeenth to early twentieth centuries, but now largely outdated. Derived from *spiauter* or *spiatter*, the names under which Portuguese cargoes of zinc were sold during the seventeenth century.

SPHALERITE. *See* BLACK JACK.

SPILLINGS. Waste material in brassmaking process. Not used locally.

SPRINGING. The operation of bringing together two ends of brass sheet to form a doubled layer, performed during the sequence of rolling standard sheet to the required gauge and size. Springing may have been used to obtain several layers to produce the very thin casing sheet in the past, but there is no record of this. Local.

STAMPS. Vertical drop hammers used for crushing. A row of vertical shafts were raised in sequence by variably placed cams on a revolving drum. A windmill was used for the purpose at Warmley and at Macclesfield, in each case to provide crushing mills for ores; but water power was commonly used for this purpose at Cornish copper mines until the nineteenth century, when steam was employed. A small set of stamps of the Cornish type, water-powered, were used at Avon Mill, Keynsham, to crush waste materials including furnace residues in order that metal could be extracted from them.

STARTS. Components of a waterwheel. The wooden or metal slats attached to the rings on which the floats or paddles were fitted.

STAYS. Metal rods attached from one paddle of a waterwheel to the next, acting as ties.

STRAIGHT AHEAD. Term denoting that rolling of metal was to be in one direction only, thus indicating that the width was not to be extended at all. Local.

STRANDED. The jamming of rolls when they were unable to take the thickness of metal fed to them. Studded meant the same. Local.

STRICK. To mark out metal to size or pattern.

STRING. Length of $\frac{1}{4}$in by $\frac{1}{4}$in brass prepared for wiredrawing processes. Commonly used at Keynsham and can be found in John Champion's Patent, No 2239 (1798), referring to wire production. Local.

STULCH or STULSH. Length of wood capped with iron at both ends, used for stopping a hammer by propping it high enough under the helve to disengage the tail end from the cogs. This was the only method of stopping a single hammer while the other two continued to work. Three hammers were powered direct from the shaft of the waterwheel with no intermediate gearing. Local.

SWIFT. Free-running reel from which wire was taken, to be drawn through a block, or wortle plate, to a drum. Local.

THOROW. Millrace, particularly a channel of water which entered a mill building. In use at Saltford, and can be found in the inventories of Warmley Company premises, 1761 (page 82). Local.

TILT HAMMER. The type of hammer normally used at brass-battery mills. The tail end was depressed by revolving cogs, carried on rings on the waterwheel shaft, and rebounded on a sunken plate. The hammer shaft pivoted on trunnions mounted in the large wooden posts near the tail end. The movement of the head was very small, only $2\frac{1}{2}$in to 5in, but at speeds of up to 360 blows per minute.

TUTENEG or TUTENAG. Alternative term for spelter (zinc), used during and prior to the eighteenth century. Believed to have an Eastern derivation.

WORK HARDENING. When brass is worked cold, by rolling, hammering, drawing or any other process, it causes a distortion in the crystalline structure of the metal which has the effect of hardening it, and making it brittle. This can be rectified by the process of annealing. *See* ANNEALING.

WORTLE PLATE. The die plate, or block, used for drawing wire. *See* BLOCK.

# Gazetteer

As far as possible, sites are placed in chronological order and numbered to correspond with the map shown below. Those sites marked * are on private property and should not be visited without permission from the owner. Most of the source material used has been annotated in the appropriate chapters, and therefore only additional references are included here.

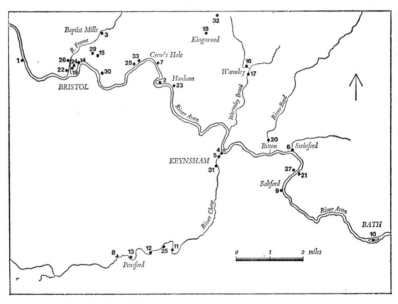

*Sites connected with the Bristol brass industry. Numbers correspond with those listed in the gazetteer*

## 1 STOCKLEY VALE COPPER WORKS (ST 563732)

This lead-smelting works, established by Sir Clement and Talbot Clerke in the late seventeenth century, is probably the site of their early experiments in the smelting of copper in the late 1680s. About 1720, John Hobbs took over the old lead-works site and again began to smelt copper there, supplying the Bristol brass company for about five years. The construction of the Portishead Railway in the 1860s is believed to have cleared the last remains from the area, now known as Nightingale Valley and on the west side of Clifton Suspension Bridge.

## 2 CONHAM COPPER WORKS (ST 629719)

Built about 1696 by Elton & Wayne on a narrow peninsula formed by a bend in the Avon, this site was about two miles upstream of Bristol Bridge, where the river was still tidal. About 1750, the works came under control of the Bristol brass company, which rebuilt and modernised the furnaces and continued smelting until the 1780s. It was leased for a period, then sold outright at the close of the century. Slag blocks and cinder are the most obvious remains, and part of the site has now been buried under a council rubbish tip.

## 3 BAPTIST MILLS (ST 602744)

The brass works, started about 1702 by Abraham Darby, were near the site of a former grist mill. Brass was produced here for manufacture under battery hammers, but later new processes were developed in the works' laboratory. This $13\frac{1}{2}$ acre site developed as the production headquarters, is said to have been abandoned by about 1814 in favour of Avon Mill, Keynsham, but still owned by the company until the 1830s. Afterwards the whole area was altered by various flood-prevention schemes (Latimer, *Annals of Bristol* (1800s)), and more recently devastated by work on the M32 Parkway Motorway. Part of the brass works, however, was centred on what is now called Millpond Street, which survives, and

possibly some of the older buildings may date from the brass-
works era. This area will lie to the east of approach roads when the
Parkway is completed, as illustrated on page 115.

### 4  AVON MILL, KEYNSHAM (ST 657689)*

The severe flooding of July 1968, followed by work of flood-
prevention schemes, has altered this site quite recently. Something
of the old brass mill can still be seen at the time of writing, particularly the small warehouse which once housed the tail-water
culverts from five of the eight undershot wheels, but it is no longer
at the water's edge as the river course has now been altered, and
the large millpond has been completely filled in. It is possible to
identify lower parts of walls of the old water-powered works, but
these are now topped by iron railings which enclose a grassed area
covering demolished buildings. The annealing cone was considered
unsafe and taken down in the early 1930s, as were other derelict
buildings about 1948. At present, plans are being discussed to build
a block of flats across this area. A pleasant row of ancillary buildings
and storehouses is left standing close to the manager's house and
the Top Yard workshops, some of which is likely to remain. This
is an ancient mill site probably dating from Domesday and recorded
as a grist mill and later a fulling mill belonging to Keynsham
Abbey in the sixteenth century.

### 5  CHEW MILL (ST 656685)

Chew Mill also belonged to Keynsham Abbey in the 1530s and
is probably a much older site. It was occupied by the brass company
in the early eighteenth century to provide power for battery hammers and this work continued until the 1870s. Emery cloth and
glass papers were produced here later, but nearer the close of the
century the mill was grinding ochre for local paint manufacturers
and is now remembered as 'the colour mill'. The derelict remains
were purchased after World War II by council authorities, and
later were made safe and tidy to form a feature in Keynsham's

Memorial Park. The 15ft diameter waterwheel still to be seen on the site is slightly smaller in size than the three used in the days of the brass mill (Appendix Two, pages 224–8).

## 6  SWINFORD MILL (ST 691689)*

John Coster took a 'double tucking mill' at Swinford in 1709, to adapt as a rolling mill for a company which later became the Joseph Percival & Copper Company, then the John Freeman & Copper Company. In 1840, under the last ownership, new premises were added, and most of the buildings which remain today appear to date from that time, as recorded by two plaques on the exterior walls. The industry continued here until 1859 when the premises were auctioned and transferred to Collingbournes, lead manufacturers, but before the end of the century were being used as a flock mill. More recently the mill has been occupied by a light engineering company, and the two 22ft 6in diameter undershot wheels have been used occasionally to generate electricity, but these are smaller in size than those recorded in the days of the copper mill (Glamorgan RO, D/Dhxr).

## 7  CREW'S HOLE COPPERWORKS (ST 627729)*

The area was usually called Screw's Hole in the early eighteenth century and the copper works referred to as the 'cupilo'. Established by at least 1710 by the Bristol brass company, there were twenty-four furnaces by 1724, and in 1754 forty-nine were seen in operation at the site. The Bristol brass company is believed to have abandoned the premises about 1881 and they were then leased to the Elton & Tyndall copper company until about 1796. Later details of occupation are not known, but during the 1820s a business of Matthews & Arnold had a brass and spelter works at Crew's Hole for about five years (Bristol Directories). In 1828 the Harfords & Bristol Brass Company sold the works and surrounding rough hilly ground and later a tar distillery was established. Troopers Hill chimney may have been part of the copper-works system of sulphur recovery, as the flues which extend to it from the smelting-works site are known to have contained deposits of sulphur when investigated early in this century. The smelting furnaces and cinder yard were enclosed in the western section of the present tar distillery, but the only recognisable remains are the copper-slag blocks in the area.

## 8 BYE MILLS AND BELTON MILLS (ST 610638)*

Bye Mills on the River Chew between Pensford and Stanton Drew was described as an iron-battery mill in 1668 (Somerset RO, DD/OB 103–5). In 1713, the Coster family leased the property and adapted it as a copper-battery mill. By the end of the eighteenth century the business, under the name of John Freeman & Copper Company, had built additional premises on the south bank of the river, which were known as Belton Mills. The industry continued here until 1860 when all equipment was auctioned. The site was later converted for use as a papermill for a few years before being closed by Bristol Water Works. The remains are now derelict and overgrown, and the watercourses are the features most easily identified with this old industrial site.

## 9 THE OLD BRASS MILL, SALTFORD (ST 687670)*

In 1721, the Bristol brass company is said to have leased a site at Saltford, formerly an old fulling mill, and erected a copper works, although later records refer specifically to a brass mill. It can be assumed that a battery mill was actually constructed, equally suitable for working copper or brass, and indeed, both metals continued to be processed by this method until 1908 when the premises housed the last brass-battery mill remaining in the country. The mill continued to roll brass sheet until 1925, but little now remains of the industry and the buildings are rapidly deteriorating. However, they do contain two annealing ovens in a more complete state than those remaining at Kelston, and thus are possibly unique in this country. There are also two undershot waterwheels, a large wheel which powered rolling equipment and a small cast-iron wheel for the grinding-stone. Two other wheel-pits can still be seen, including the one used to power the battery mill. The remaining watercourses are also of interest.

## 10 WESTON MILL, BATH (ST 724649)*

This mill was established by 1729, and possibly earlier, as suggested by Twerton Parish Church registers of local Dutch workers. It is noted on Thorpe's Map of Bath in 1742 and, in 1801, Warner referred to the industry in his *History of Bath* as being 'where masses of brass and copper are flattened, and drawn out into furnaces, sugar-bakers' pans, and other implements', suggesting that the premises had a similar function to those at Saltford. By 1813, the mill had been taken over by a business producing edge-tools but by 1840 had been converted to a log-wood mill. It was situated at the upper Twerton weir, half way along Dutch Island but no remains can now be seen. A small brass foundry, where the author's grandfather once worked, was established later on the island. It was not connected in any way with the Bristol industry, but this works has caused some confusion in distinguishing the original brass-works site.

## 11 WOODBOROUGH MILL (ST 636642)*

Sited on the River Chew between Woollard and Compton Dando, this mill was described as a tucking mill in the sixteenth century. In 1736, John Light leased the premises from the Popham family, and by then they were already described as 'three brass kettle mills or brass battery mills . . . heretofore being two water grist mills under one roof'. The lease was almost certainly on behalf of the Bristol brass company, which is known to have been working this site for a period in the eighteenth century. By the 1790s it was described as derelict, and early in the following century, was used as a tannery for a short period, then later as a grist mill up to World War II. It is now taken over as a farm building

N

but the mill premises still remain and the watercourse can still be traced, cutting across a large bend in the river.

### 12   PUBLOW MILL (ST 625642)*

By 1731, the Coster family had taken over a former iron or plate mill at Publow, at one time described as a frying-pan works. The premises were converted for rolling copper, but later copper refining was also carried out and batteryware was made here. Several older inhabitants of the area tell of memories handed down of the River Chew being used to transport horse-drawn barges, possibly by the copper company between adjacent mill sites on the river. The industry ceased in 1860 when all equipment was auctioned, and the site reverted to farm use with some of the mill buildings being adapted. It is now known as Church Farm. From these premises traces of the mill race can be seen stretching across the fields to Publow Bridge. At this bridge, one of the keystones bears the inscription 'J F & CO 1799', referring to the John Freeman & Copper Company, the name of the business in its final stages.

### 13   PENSFORD MILL (ST 618637)

Pensford Mill was leased to the Coster copper concern by at least the 1730s, but the premises continued to be rented for use as a grist mill when the mill house was adapted as a copper warehouse, an arrangement which continued until the early nineteenth century. The lease may have been acquired in order to control the use of water for Publow Mill downstream, or possibly to obtain navigation rights between Bye Mills and Publow. Pensford Mill continued to work as a grist mill almost until the twentieth century.

### 14   THE BRASS WAREHOUSE, QUEEN STREET, BRISTOL (ST 593730)*

This large building backed on to the river at a site just above Bristol Bridge, with a frontage in Queen Street, off Castle Street.

The earliest records so far discovered are on John Rocque's map of Bristol, 1746, although it may have been established earlier. Bristol Directory entries include it as the commercial headquarters of the Harfords & Bristol Brass Company until 1812, and a large corn-milling factory now stands on the site. From St Phillip's Bridge, looking towards Bristol Bridge, copper-slag blocks can still be seen built into the riverside walls of the mill, indicating the old wharf of the brass warehouse.

## 15 BABERS TOWER, BRISTOL (ST 598732)*

References in the Minutes of Bristol Common Council suggest that William Champion carried out his zinc-smelting experiments and early production of metallic zinc at Babers Tower, just off Old Market. The premises were situated on the corner lying between the streets now known as Jacob Street, Unity Street and Midland Road. Champion was reprimanded by the council for causing a common nuisance at these premises in 1742, and the following year he reported that the works had then been destroyed. The site is vacant at the time of writing, with no apparent remains to be seen of its important industrial history.

## 16 WARMLEY WORKS (ST 670728)*

William Champion formed his company in 1746, and by 1748 the Warmley works was involved in a new kind of comprehensive production, smelting zinc and copper, and producing brass and manufacturing wares, all at this same site. His production of zinc was the first large-scale commercial production to be carried out in Europe. A year later a Newcomen steam engine was installed to recycle water used for powering the waterwheels back to the newly constructed millpond, adopting a technique that had been recently introduced elsewhere. Expansion was continuous, and by 1761 a windmill for crushing ores was being used at Warmley; the tower can still be seen there. By 1767, a large pin factory had been erected, possibly the clock-tower building saved from demolition within recent years. Pinmaking and zinc production continued until the mid-nineteenth century but later the site was taken over to produce salt-glazed stoneware. Champion's house is now used as offices for the urban district council, but the site of his large millpond has been filled in to provide hard standing for caravans. A statue of Neptune, once at the lake's centre, remains, rather mutilated and covered with ivy; the gatehouse over Warmley Brook at the entrance to the millpond site still stands, largely constructed of rectangular copper-slag blocks. During 1972, the UDC created a small Champion Park directly opposite the clock-tower building, appropriately surrounded by copper-slag coping blocks on the walls, creating a well-deserved memorial to the pioneer industry which once existed in the surrounding 79 acres.

### 17  HOLE LANE WORKS (ST 671725)

The one brief reference to the use of this site is quoted by Hamilton in his *English Brass and Copper Industries* in a list of mills once belonging to the Bristol company, compiled by the last manager at Keynsham, A. C. V. Davies. A mill site in Hole Lane, now Mill Lane, is very close to Warmley Works and it may have been taken over by the old Bristol brass company as part of the Warmley Works' 79 acres, and possibly used only for a very short period. The derelict remains of the mill, including a large number of copper-slag blocks survived until 1971, situated between the Mill Lane Methodist Chapel and Warmley Brook, but the recent rebuilding of a new bridge over the brook has left nothing recognisable.

### 18  THE CUPOLA, KINGSWOOD (ST 652741)

The site of the new copper furnaces constructed by William Champion in 1761, which he described as his Upper Works near the centre of Kingswood, is marked on the Tithe Map of 1844 as 'the Cupola', the traditional name for copper furnaces. Braine's *Kingswood Forest*, page 215, refers to a tower near this site said to be 55ft high, which may have been an additional windmill for the purpose of crushing ores, similar to the one remaining at Warmley. No obvious remains have been discovered to link the area with the copper industry, but part of the works are said to have been demolished to provide stone for the local church (Bristol Reference Library, Ellacombe MSS, Vol 8, 46).

### 19  THE COUNTING HOUSE, SMALL STREET, BRISTOL (ST 588731)

The committee meetings of the Joseph Percival & Copper Company were held at The Three Tuns hostelry in Corn Street until 2 September 1762, when the first meeting was recorded at the company's Compting House in Small Street. After the business became the John Freeman & Copper Company, this remained the official address until 1865, when the Bristol General Post Office was erected on the site.

### 20  BITTON MILL (ST 682698)*

References to a brass works at Bitton have not been discovered, prior to the sales notices of March 1769, of sites belonging to the Warmley Company. The Bristol brass company appear to have continued the works as a brass-battery mill until about 1825. It was then taken over by paper manufacturers who had occupied premises further upstream on the River Boyd, and under a different ownership this industry was to continue into the twentieth century. The site now produces fibreboard, but plans are in hand to drain the large millpond to prevent flooding, and subsequently to move the works. The pond dates from the days of the brass works and is probably the closest link still remaining at the site.

### 21  KELSTON MILLS (ST 694679)*

As with Bitton Mill, this site does not appear in records until the sales notice of the Warmley Company, then described as a copper forge and brass manufactory. The lease later passed into the hands of the Bristol brass company which continued to use it as a battery mill until the late 1840s. In 1855 a surveyor's report recorded that the site had been unoccupied for several years (Glos RO, D1628, 3 May 1955). It is now badly overgrown and dangerous, but five watercourses can still be seen and the two tall stacks of the annealing furnaces which unfortunately lack the interior linings. Several dates and flood-lines can be found carved on the stonework, together with names or initials of workers in families known to have once been employed at Kelston.

## 22 ST AUGUSTINE'S BACK WAREHOUSE AND FOUNDRY (ST 586730)

This warehouse was first referred to in the sales notice of the Warmley Company, but apparently was not taken over by the Bristol brass company as other sites were. Two years later, property at St Augustine's Back, opposite the drawbridge, was again advertised for sale (*Bristol Journal*, 30 March 1771) consisting of two houses and land on which was a newly erected commodious warehouse and brass foundry, with entrances to Denmark Street and Orchard Street. One of the houses was tenanted by James Matthews, formerly a minor partner and probably an employee of the Warmley Company. No further information has been discovered, and no remains can be identified.

## 23 HANHAM SPELTER WORKS (ST 635718)

James Emerson established works for smelting zinc and making brass by the direct method about half a mile upstream from Conham, in the 1770s. Writing in 1786, Watson misspelt the name as Henham which has been widely copied ever since (see *Hamilton, The English Brass and Copper Industries*). After Emerson's bankruptcy in 1803 the works was occupied by Philip George who continued the smelting of zinc, and was taken over later by Christopher Pope. The premises were advertised as going concern in 1838 (*Bristol Mirror*, 27 October 1838), but it is doubtful if they were occupied afterwards. Part of the site has been destroyed by local quarrying and part has been buried by the spoil heap from Hanham Colliery, but it is said that fragmentary remains can still be found in the undergrowth.

## 24 THE COUNTING HOUSE AND WAREHOUSE, CORN STREET (ST 589730)

These premises were the commercial headquarters of the Harfords & Bristol Brass Company, and may have been a warehouse taken over from the old Bristol brass company. An advertisement appeared in the *Bristol Gazette*, 13 February 1800, for brass melters who were directed to apply to the office, opposite the exchange in Corn Street. Later, with the disposal of much of the company's property, only part of these premises were occupied, the remainder being leased out to William Beloe & Company, sugar brokers. The entire property was eventually sold in 1861 by the Harford company for £6,000 to the National Provincial Bank which still occupies the site under the name of National Westminster Bank (Glos RO, D1628, Statement of Sale of Property in Corn Street, etc).

## 25 WOOLLARD MILL (ST 632644)*

This grist mill was adapted in the 1730s as a rolling mill to produce tinplate and continued this work until the 1770s. In the early 1780s the site was taken over by the copper-smelting business of Isaac Elton and Thomas Tyndall, where they rolled copper for about ten years. By the mid 1790s, the John Freeman & Copper Company had acquired the lease of the mill, adjacent to their three other sites on the river. This was not forfeited until just prior to 1860, when the machinery and effects were auctioned with those of the other local sites. The mill is now a private dwelling house, but traces of the weir and an industrial building can still be seen in the garden, and the culverts which contained the mill race still remain in the cellars of the house.

## 26 LEWINS MEAD WIRE MANUFACTORY (ST 587733)

From at least the early 1780s, John Champion, son of William Champion, was concerned in Young's Corn Mill in Lewins Mead which housed a Wasborough steam engine. Warehouses owned by the Champion family were situated nearby, and subsequently these properties were adapted by John Champion to produce brass and iron wire by means of steam-driven equipment, after Boulton & Watt had converted the engine by fitting a separate condenser. The wireworks were taken over by Philip George in 1799, and occupied by him until at least 1812. The location in Lewins Mead has not been established precisely, but as the premises backed on to the River Frome they were probably on or adjacent to the present site of Froomsbridge House.

## 27 THE OLD LEATHER MILL, SALTFORD (ST 692679)

During the late 1780s, the Bristol brass company acquired a two-thirds share of a paper mill, formerly a leather mill, on the opposite bank of the River Avon to the mill at Kelston. Just after the turn of the century the remaining third share was taken over by the Harford company at a time when sites were being disposed of, but possibly it was thought worthwhile to acquire the water rights for the whole width of the weir. The site was never used as a brass mill and allowed to become derelict, while the mill house was rented out and later used as an inn. This still remains as The Jolly Sailor (Glos RO, D1628) (Appendix Two, page 225).

## 28 NETHAM BRASS WORKS, BRISTOL (ST 616727)

From about 1800, a watermill at Netham was occupied by the business of Anderson, New & Company for the purpose of brass manufacture. In 1809 the company, by then called Pitt, Anderson Birch & Company, was involved in an action at Gloucester assizes against the Bristol Dock Company for loss of use of the premises, caused by the new Bristol dock developments. The company was awarded £10,000, but went out of existance before the 1820s, and there was no further connection between the brass industry and the premises at Netham. There are no recognisable remains.

## 29 REDCROSS STREET WAREHOUSE, BRISTOL (approx ST 597733)

The commercial headquarters and warehouse of Anderson, New & Company is to be found in Bristol Directories from 1800, in Redcross Street, near Old Market. The premises were taken over when the business became Pitt, Anderson, Birch & Company after 1807, but directory entries are discontinued after 1818, when listed as Pitt, Savage, Wiltshire & Company, a business which also had premises at the Broad Quay. The precise positions of these sites are not known.

## 30 CHEESE LANE WORKS, BRISTOL (approx ST 597727)

Bristol Directories indicate that iron and brass-wire works of Philip George, junior, moved to new premises at Cheese Lane by 1812. By 1815 the products of this company were described as copper, spelter, wire, patent zinc and iron, but these same goods were being listed under the name of Christopher Pope from 1821. His premises were described as Avon Mill, St Phillips, but were advertised as situated in Cheese Lane, after Pope's bankruptcy in 1832. The business continued under the same name until 1844, when the directory entries ceased. The property was positioned between Cheese Lane and the river, but the exact location is not known and it is not possible, therefore, to identify any remains which may exist.

## 31 SOUTH MILL, KEYNSHAM (ST 656679)*

South Mill was described as a cotton mill from the late eighteenth century, but some time after 1811, the Harfords & Bristol Brass Company purchased the premises and leased them to a flax dresser (Glos RO, D1628). Probably the company wished to acquire water rights to ensure power for the Chew Mill battery works at the next site downstream. The property was advertised in the *Bristol Mirror*, 18 June 1831, and the brass company sold it shortly after. When the mill changed hands in 1833, it was described as a new flour mill. In the early 1870s the building was involved in a disastrous fire and soon afterwards was adapted again to a new industry of grinding imported dyewoods. Later the name was changed to the Albert Mill, and its dyewood business survived until quite recent times.

## 32 SOUNDWELL WORKS (ST 660751)

At the bankruptcy sale of Christopher Pope's Soundwell premises in February 1832, they were described as having been built for spelter and brass manufacture at enormous expense within the previous ten years. No information has been discovered about the later use of this well-equipped works. Modern factories now occupy the site and no remains exist to link it directly with the brass and spelter industry, but the embankments can still be seen of the nearby Bristol & Gloucestershire Railway mentioned in Pope's advertisement (page 135). The widely scattered copper-slag blocks used in the buildings of this area could possibly be connected with the Cupola works at Kingswood (Gazetteer 18) rather than the works at Soundwell.

## 33 BLACKSWARTH LANE WORKS (ST 619730)

A large number of copper-slag blocks in the walls between road and riverside in an area of Blackswarth Lane, indicates the site of what was primarily a lead works. But the St George Tithe Map of 1845 refers to a section of these premises as an old brass works belonging to Joseph Mosely which, by this time, was no longer in use.

## COPPER-SLAG BLOCKS

Remains of the copper-smelting industry can be seen in many parts of Bristol and its surroundings, in black building blocks made of copper slag. Most common, are the triangular coping stones used for topping walls such as those along the Bath Road in the vicinity of Arno's Vale and Flowers Hill; at Tower Road, Warmley, surrounding the Kelston estate; and in numerous other places.

Half-round coping blocks are less common, but can be seen around Ashton Court Estate and approaching Bitton from Bristol, or in the vicinity of Warmley House.

Rectangular blocks built into walls exist in large numbers in Blackswarth Road, and further on in Conham Vale. Much of Black Castle in Arno's Vale is constructed of this material, including some shaped blocks in the circular towers. (William Reeve, who built the castle, married into the Harford family and was connected with the Bristol brass company.) Other examples can be seen in many of the brass-mill remains, particularly those of the old Bristol company and also of the Warmley Company.

As well as in villages in the immediate vicinity of Bristol, many of the rectangular blocks can be seen in the small towns and villages on the banks of the Severn and Wye, giving rise to the suggestion that this material may have been used as ballast for coastal and inland-water transport.

Rectangular blocks of similar dimensions, apart from a slight difference in average height of about $\frac{1}{2}$in, can be seen in the areas where the Cheadle brass company was active. Slag can also be seen in the Swansea area, but more often it is broken pieces, and the dimensions do not conform with the blocks found at Bristol and Cheadle.

Many Bristol examples have disappeared in quite recent road-widening and development schemes, but these black lustrous blocks are extremely durable and can look very attractive. Those that remain are worth keeping.

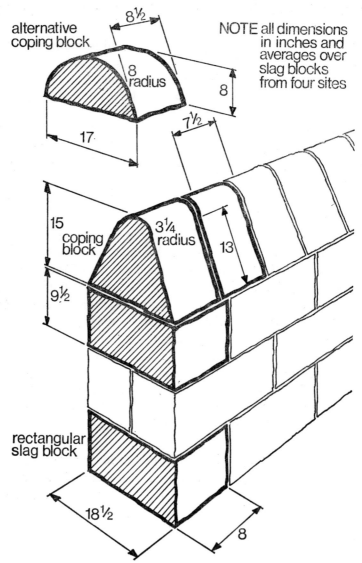

*Types of slag blocks to be found in the Bristol area*

# Purchases of Cornish Copper Ore

INFORMATION compiled from notebooks of the Morris Lockwood Company, Swansea, National Library of Wales, MSS 15101–9.

### TABLE 1

*Ore purchased by John Coster & Co on behalf of:*
Brass Warehouse Co (Bristol brass company, smelting at Crew's Hole)
Elton & Co (Elton & Wayne, smelting at Conham)
Eng Co (English Copper Company, smelting at Lower Redbrook)
All bought small individual amounts in addition to these joint purchases, particularly the English Copper Company, and Elton & Wayne.

| 1729 | 1730 | | | 1731 | | | 1732 | | |
|------|------|-----|-----|------|-----|-----|------|-----|-----|
| tons | tons | cwt | qr | tons | cwt | qr | tons | cwt | qr |
| 627 | 1,198 | 20 | 2 | 1,069 | 18 | 0 | 544 | 10 | 2 |

The joint purchases then ceased. John Coster had died during 1731.

*They continued individually* (parts of a ton ignored):

| | 1733 | 1734 | 1735 | 1736 | 1737 |
|------|------|------|------|------|------|
| | tons | tons | tons | tons | tons |
| Brass Warehouse Co* | 1,242 | 1,474 | 1,401 | 1,689 | 874 |
| Eng Copr Compy | 375 | 1,209 | 830 | 470 | 794 |
| Elton & Co† | 242 | 169 | 489 | 360 | 232 |
| Coster & Co‡ | 36 | — | 731 | 338 | 636 |

* Believed to be also receiving ore from own company mines.
† Believed to be also receiving ore from Wicklow, Ireland.
‡ Carried on by Thomas Coster until 1739, smelting at Melyncryddan, Neath, for a short period. Became Joseph Percival & Copper Company during 1740s.

## TABLE 2

*Estimated yield of copper from assay of purchased ore (purchases in tons, parts of a ton ignored for clarity):*

| Company | Purchases and yields | Year | | | | | |
|---|---|---|---|---|---|---|---|
| | | *1745* | *1748* | *1749* | *1750* | *1751* | *1752* |
| | | tons | tons | tons | tons | tons | tons |
| Brass Warehouse Co | ore purchased | 2,770 | 2,590 | 998 | 1,679 | 1,769 | 3,020 |
| | estimated yield | 440 | 350 | 156 | 287 | 284 | 422 |
| Jos Percival & Co* | ore purchased | 1,362 | 1,816 | 1,428 | 2,552 | 2,016 | 2,318 |
| | estimated yield | 148 | 213 | 186 | 349 | 290 | 302 |
| Wm Champion & Co† | ore purchased | — | 516 | 491 | 662 | 608 | 646 |
| | estimated yield | — | 81 | 66 | 63 | 66 | 79 |

No records for Elton & Wayne (see Table 1) are included after 1744 when 160 tons of ore was purchased.

* Formerly Coster & Co. By these dates was smelting at White Rock, Swansea, and still manufacturing in the Bristol area.

† Company established 1746 and started operations in 1748.

| Company | Purchases and yields | Year | | | | | |
|---------|---------|------|------|------|------|------|------|
| | | *1765* | *1766* | *1767* | *1768* | *1769* | *1770* |
| | | tons | tons | tons | tons | tons | tons |
| Brass Warehouse (Wire) Co* | ore purchased | 2,854 | 3,735 | 2,542 | 4,110 | 4,902 | 6,002 |
| | estimated yield | 384 | 523 | 343 | 530 | 562 | 791 |
| John Freeman & Co† | ore purchased | 2,570 | 3,107 | 3,362 | 3,930 | 4,031 | 3,931 |
| | estimated yield | 297 | 339 | 373 | 422 | 457 | 424 |
| Wm Champion & Co‡ | ore purchased | 3,120 | 2,816 | 2,806 | 779 | — | — |
| | estimated yield | 365 | 346 | 289 | 76 | — | — |
| Elton & Co§ | ore purchased | — | — | — | — | — | 369 |
| | estimated yield | — | — | — | — | — | 40 |

\* Brass Warehouse Co is referred to as Brass Wire Co from 1768.
† John Freeman & Co, formerly Joseph Percival & Co.
‡ Wm Champion & Co, otherwise the Warmley Company.
§ Elton & Co, believed to be Isaac Elton and Thomas Tyndall.

# The 1862 Sales Catalogue of Sites

VALUABLE FREEHOLD MILLS, MACHINERY, AND FREE-HOLD HOUSES AND LAND, MIDWAY BETWEEN BRISTOL AND BATH, SITUATE AT KEYNSHAM AND SALTFORD, IN THE COUNTY OF SOMERSET, KNOWN AS "HARFORDS' & THE BRISTOL BRASS BATTERY & WIRE COMPANY'S WORKS", Possessing unusual advantages of position and approach, by excellent Roads, by Water on the Kennet and Avon Canal, and by the Great Western Railway: Stations of which latter adjoin the principal Mills, TO BE SOLD BY AUCTION, WITHOUT RESERVE . . . ON TUESDAY, THE 11th DAY OF FEBRUARY, 1862.

LOT 1 COMPRISES THE WORKS AT KEYNSHAM
Containing Metal Furnaces, Annealing Ovens, Rolling, Metal Sheathing, Metal Tube, Wire Drawing, Grinding, and Battery Mills, Machinery, and Tools, driven by 15* Water Wheels, and 1 Ten-Horse Power Steam Engine. Also, the Managers's Residence, Gardens, Cottages, and Land. Also, THE WORKS AT SALTFORD, Which include Rolling and Brass Battery Mills, Machinery and Tools, driven by 4 powerful Water Wheels. Also Cottages, Gardens, and Land.

The Works at Keynsham and Saltford have an abundant and very extensive Right of Water on the Rivers Avon and Chew.

As Manufacturing Works, the above may be justly ranked amongst the most eligible in the Kingdom, to which are attached Commercial connexions of the very highest character, commanding a lucrative trade that has been carried on for upwards of a Century by the present and late Firms of Harfords and the Bristol Brass Battery and Wire Company.

The whole of this lot is Freehold, and including the site of the Mills, Houses, Cottages, Gardens, Mill Ponds, and Land contains about 13 Acres.

Schedules of the costly Machinery and Tools, comprehending everything necessary for the conduct of an extensive Business, and WHICH WILL BE SOLD WITH THE PROPERTY IN ONE LOT, are appended.

The present Occupier's Tenancy expires on 25th March next, at which time Possession will be given to a purchaser.

LOTS 2 and 3 Comprise the SITE OF THE OLD LEATHER MILLS, with their reputed Rights of Water, House, Gardens, and Land, all Freehold, and containing in the whole upwards of 2 Acres. All other particulars with orders to view, can be obtained of Mr Edwin Naish, Bristol; or of Messrs. Osborne, Ward & Co., No 41, Broad Street, Bristol, the Vendors' Solicitors.

SCHEDULES of MACHINERY and TOOLS COMPRISED IN LOT 1.

SCHEDULE A, at KEYNSHAM ROLLING and WIRE MILLS.

STABLE.—Water Trough and Stable Fittings.

MILLWRIGHT'S SHOP.—3 Benches, 3 ditto Vices, 1 Cast Iron Lathe and Wheel, 1 Foot Lathe, 1 Iron Stove and Pipe, 1 Grindstone and Frame.

SMITH'S SHOP, No 1.—Two Forges with Water-troughs complete, 2 pairs of Bellows, 2 Anvils, 3 Bench Vices, 1 Forge Crane, 1 Bick Iron, 1 Swage Anvil, Grindstone and Frame, Forge Tools, 1 Press Drill, Screw Cutter Frame and Dies.

SMITH'S SHOP, No 2.—1 Lathe and Wheel complete, Bench, 2 Bench Vices, 1 Forge with Bellows and Troughs, Stamp for setting Cutter Plates, 1 Anvil, pair of Hand Shears, pair of spare Spindles, 2 sets of Splitters, 1 large pair of Slitter Spindles with 3 sets of Blades, Smith's Tools, various old Taps, and Dies and pair of Stocks for same, and 3 old Mandrills.

WAREHOUSE.—Patent Weighing Machine, various Weights—in all about 3 tons and 8 cwt, various.

WIRE ANNEALING HOUSE, No 1.—3 Ovens, 3 Carriages, 9 Waggons, and Fire Tools.

PICKLING HOUSE.—2 Wood Water Troughs and 1 Lead Cistern.

WOOD HOUSE.—1 spare Iron Spar Wheel and Shaft with Wood Cogs, 2 smaller ditto, ditto with Iron Cogs and 3 spare Annealing Waggons for the Rolling Mills.

O

ANNEALING HOUSE, No 2.—One Annealing oven and one Carriage.

WAREHOUSE UNDER.—Beam and Scales, Iron Flooring Plates, one Wrought Iron Shaft, 2 Coupling Boxes, 3 Carriages and Brasses.

ROUND HOUSE.—2 Annealing Ovens, 6 Waggons, 1 Carriage, Fire Tools, 12 Mill Waggons, 1 large ditto, Iron Flooring Plates, 2 pairs of Hand Shares and Blocks.

LATTEN ROLLING MILLS.—One Water Wheel 18ft.×3ft 6in. with an 18 feet Fly Wheel, Shafting and Driving Wheels, 2 pairs Rolls 3ft.6in. and 2ft.6in. wide, Cast Iron Bed and Wrought Iron Pillars with the Spanners to fit.

One Water Wheel 16ft.×2ft. Shafting and Gearing driving 4 pair of Shears. Crab Winch, Sheave Blocks and Chains.

WIRE SLIP ROLLING MILLS.—Two water Wheels 18ft.×3ft. Shafting and Driving Wheels, driving 1 pair of Wire Slip Rolls, pair of Grove Rolls 18in. Bed and Pillars, one Grove Roll 24in., Spanners for Roll Beds, Grindstone, Iron Incline for Slips, one long Annealing Oven, one short Annealing Oven, Fire Tools, Oven Carriage, 3 Waggons, Iron Flooring Plates, Water Trough, and Eight-day Clock.

WIRE MILL, No 1—Water Wheel 18ft.×4ft., Shafting and Wheels driving 8 Wire blocks down Stairs, with the requisite Reels and Shafting, Spur and Bevil Wheels affixed to Cast Iron Table Frame complete, 4 Scale Beams and Balances, and 20 Wire Blocks, with the necessary Reels, Shafting, Bevil and Spur Wheels affixed to Wood Table, Iron Stoves, Fire Tools, Straightening Bench with Screws, Vice and Tongues, Bench Shears, Grindstone and Frame, Pair of Scale Beams, Iron Mortar, spare Cast Roll Bed, Wrought Iron Pillars and Carriages, Grindstone, 7 Scale Beams and Carriages, Stove Hand Shears, Anvil and Bench Frame.

COLOMINE MILL†—Water Wheel 18ft.×2ft.3in. driving 3 pairs of Stones, completely fixed with strong Cast Iron Framing attached, from top floor is a Shaft, Gearing, and Cylinder, for turning latten bright; A Large Wood Trough, 2 Spare Cylinders, Lot of Wood Patterns, Grindstone.

SLITTING MILL.—Water Wheel 13ft.6in.×2ft.10in., with powerful

Shafting and Gearing driving Slitter; Pair of Runners about 5ft. for grinding, and pair of Slitters on Strong Cast Iron Bed, with Wrought Iron Pillars and Brasses.

WIRE MILL, No 2.—Water Wheel 19ft.×2ft.10in, Shafting and Gearing, driving 3 pairs Grove Rolls on Iron Beds, and Framing and Wire Block, Wood Bench and Framing down Stairs, and 15 Wire Blocks with the requisite Shafting and Bevil Wheels, on 3 Wood Benches and Framing, 5 Scale Beams and Balances, Iron Stove, Wood Work Bench and spare Grove Roll Bed, Small Grove Roll, Bevil Wheels and Shafting upstairs.

OLD YARD.—Pump, Boat, Cast Water Wheel Stake, 4 Mandrill, 2 Centre Pieces for Water Wheels, Ladder, Wharf Crane, and Turret Clock; all the Shop Lamps.

TUBE SHOP.—2 Soldering Stones, 2 Cast Iron Lathes for turning Battery, and all the Shop Lamps.

IN THE TURNERY.—Iron Stove, 2 Grindstones and Frames, 4 Anvils and Blocks, Shears, Hammers and Tools, Soldering Forge and Bellows.

BATTERY WAREHOUSE.—Iron Stove and Pipe, Beam and Scales, Wood Desk, Iron and Bick.

GENERAL WAREHOUSE.—4 Beams and Scales, 3 Sledges, 2 Shruff Blocks and Wood Desk.

SHRUFF WAREHOUSE.—Beam and Scales, and one Shruff Block.

SMITH'S SHOP.—2 Forges, 2 Iron Troughs, 3 pair Bellows, Forge Crane, 1 Bench, 2 Vices, Fire Grate Anvil, Square ditto, Swage ditto, Bick Iron, 4 Mandrills, Grindstone and Frame, Iron Pump and Smith's Tools.

METAL HOUSE, No 3.—2 Fire Engines with Leather Hose, &c., complete.

## AT KEYNSHAM BATTERY MILLS

BATTERY MILL, No 1.—Water Wheel 16ft.×2ft.4ins., with Cast Iron Shaft and Gearing, driving 3 Hammers, 208 Hammers,‡ 57 Anvils, 9 Hursks, 13 Tail Rings 12 Shill Irons, Tail Plates, 4 Hand Shears, 1 Block, 1 Annealing Oven, 1 Carriage, 2 Waggons, Scales and Beam, and Fire Tools.

BATTERY MILL, No 2.—Water Wheel Wood Shaft, 16ft.×2ft.4ins., and Gearing, driving 3 Hammers, 13 Hammers, 4 Anvils, 4 Hursks and Tail Plates, 6 Tail Rings, 8 Shill Irons, 1 Vice, Iron Water Trough, 1 Annealing Oven, 1 Carriage, 2 Waggons, Sundry Fire Tools, Scales and Beam.

BATTERY MILL, No 3.—Water Wheel 16ft.×2ft.4ins., Cast Iron Shaft, driving 3 Hammers, 250 Hammers, 54 Anvils, 9 Hursks, 11 Tail Rings and Plates, 10 Shill Irons, 6 Hand Shears, 2 Blocks, 1 Annealing Oven, 1 Carriage, 2 Waggons, Scales and Beam, and Fire Tools.

SHED.—Water Wheel, with Wrought Iron Shaft and Framing, 9ft.× 1ft.3in, driving grindstone


## AT SALTFORD ROLLING AND BATTERY MILLS.

BATTERY MILL, No 1.—Water Wheel 15ft.×3ft.6ins., Wood Shaft and Gearing, driving 3 Hammers, 245 Hammers, 48 Anvils, 8 Hursks, 14 Tail Rings, 14 Shill Irons, 9 Tail Plates, 2 Scales and Beams, Vice and Stock, Hand Shears, one Annealing Oven, 1 Carriage, 2 Waggons, Fire Tools, Wood Bench.

BATTERY MILL, No 2.—Water Wheel 15ft.×3ft.6ins., Wood Shaft and Gearing, driving 3 Hammers, 199 Hammers, 36 Anvils, 8 Hursks, 9 Tail Rings, 7 Tail Plates, 9 Shill Irons, Scales and Beam, 2 Hand Shears and Blocks, 1 Annealing Oven, 1 Carriage, 2 Waggons, Wood Benches, and Fire Tools.

ROLLING MILL.—Water Wheel 15ft.×3ft.6in., Wood Shaft and Gearing and Water Wheel 15ft.×3ft.6ins., driving 3 pair Shears and 2 pairs Rolls, 5ft.6ins. and 3ft.6ins. wide, with Beds and Pillars complete, Spanners, 7 Trolleys, Blocks and Fall, large Scales and Beam, Hand Shears, 2 Annealing Ovens, 2 Carriages, 6 Waggons, Fire Tools.

OUTSIDE AND YARD.—Water Wheel, Iron Shaft, and Wrought Iron Frame, driving Grindstone, 1 Boat.


## SCHEDULE B. AT KEYNSHAM ROLLING AND WIRE MILLS.

SMITH'S SHOP, No 2.—1 pair Slitter Spindle, with one set of Blades, 3 Stocks, with Taps and Dies complete.

POT MAKING ROOM.—2 Iron Stoves and Pipes.

PICKLING HOUSE,—Stove Plate, 4 Lead Cisterns, Lead Pump, and one Drying Stove.

STORE ROOM ADJOINING ANNEALING-HOUSE, No 2.—1 Stove and Pipe.

LATTEN ROLLING MILLS.—1 pair of long Shears and Driving Gear.

WIRE SLIP ROLLING MILLS,—1 pair of Wire Slip Rolls, with Iron Beds and Pillars, 1 Iron Role [Roll] Bed and Pillars.

COUNTING HOUSE.—2 Mahogany Desks.

NEW WORKS. Right Hand Entrance.—Iron Stove and Pipes, Wash Tub, Iron Bedstead.

METAL HOUSE, No 1.—4 Iron Bedsteads, 1 ditto Trough, 1 ditto Stone, Iron Rests, and Fire Tools.

METAL HOUSE, No 2.—2 Iron Bedsteads, 2 Water Troughs, Fire Tools and Rests, all the sets of Moulds and Clips, Cast Iron Cutting Stand, and the Tools for same.

TUBE SHOP.—Work Bench, 4 Bench Vices, Bench, 2 Charging ditto, 2 Iron Drawing Benches, 3 Wood ditto, Stone and Bench Tools, Hydraulic proving Pump, Lead Pickling Trough, Water Trough, 2 Steam Boilers, Bench and Vice, Pestle and Mortar, Iron Stove and Pipe, One High Pressure 10-Horse Engine complete, with the whole of the Wrought Iron Shafting, Pulleys, Brackets, Brasses, and Gearing, driving Face Plate, 2 Tube Drawing Machines, Circular Saw, pair Shears, and 12 Wire Blocks, Iron Stove and Pipe, 7 Benches, 6 Bench Vices, Straightening Bench and Block, pair Hand Shears, Grindstone, Scale Beam and Balance, Iron Hang-Downs, and Tube drawing Tools, two powerful Wire Blocks, and one Cast Iron Lathe.

IN THE YARD.—Cast Iron Lamp Post and River Water Pump.

* An incorrect number. There were eight wheels at Avon Mill, and three driving wheels and one grinding wheel at Chew Mill. See subsequent schedules.

† Calamine Mill.

‡ This item should read hammer-heads, similarly in following paragraphs.

# *Acknowledgements*

WHEN, eight years ago, Dr Angus Buchanan and Neil Cossons started to organise a series of courses on industrial archaeology, one of their first tasks was to encourage students to make their own inquiries into the history of local industries. I am grateful for the inspiration which they provided, for this book developed from the results of those initial inquiries.

At first, it seemed that there was a dearth of printed material available for consultation, but it was possible to find elderly local residents who remembered their work at the Keynsham and Saltford brass mills. I was particularly indebted to the late Mr J. Exon, Mr Harry Barnett, Mr A. E. Shellard, and most of all to Mr Tom Shellard for telling me of their working days there. Miss Ethel Gane had interesting memories of her father, and Mrs G. Watts of her grandfather. Miss Doris Brock, the late Mrs Rawlings and other members of the Ollis family allowed me to copy their photographs. Members of the Keynsham & Saltford Local History Society later made valuable contributions to the local material being collated, especially Miss Mary Fairclough, Mrs Nan Benfield, Mrs Connie Smith and her daughter Mary, Mr R. Scott, Mr P. Sims and the late Mr George Fray of Birmingham who compiled a great deal of information on the history of his family.

It soon became apparent that there was a large amount of information to be gained at record offices and reference libraries in various parts of the country, and I have to thank the staff of all these establishments for their valuable assistance, but that received from the local library at Keynsham has been particularly helpful.

I am indebted to Mr M. C. E. Bird the librarian, to his assistants, and to those who operate the Somerset County inter-library loan service.

It was essential to discover something of the techniques of the industry which I had chosen to investigate. As a housewife, with no technical training, I became very grateful for the existence of the Historical Metallurgy Group and for those members who are professionally concerned with their subjects and yet able to explain the techniques involved in terms which a layman can understand. Dr R. F. Tylecote, Mr Keith Gale and the late Mr R. G. Morton were all outstanding in this respect. I have also to thank Mr P. C. Thornton of Bath University of Technology, Mr D. Morgan Rees of the National Museum of Wales, Mr S. W. K. Morgan of Imperial Smelting Processes Ltd, and Dr R. A. Mott from Sheffield for help with specific technical queries.

With the founding of BIAS (the Bristol Industrial Archaeological Society), I received help from several members on local information and source material. Mrs Dorothy Vintner, Mr Robin Stiles, Mr Humphrey H. Lloyd, Mr M. J. H. Southway, Mr J. H. Bettey and Mr A. E. Woolrich all provided information of interest. Mr George Watkins made a particularly valuable contribution in allowing me access to notes he made twenty-five to thirty years ago when visiting remains of the brass mills, in talking to the old brass workers, and in corresponding with Mr A. C. V. Davies, the last manager at the mills. Mr Watkins has also kindly allowed me to make use of photographs he took at this time, and Mr L. R. Reeves loaned me postcards from his extensive collection. In Bath, Mrs C. Turner and Mr M. Messer gave help with details on the industry at Weston Mill, and with notes from Twerton Parish Church registers.

When I was carrying out research on the development of the industry in other parts of the country, Professor J. R. Harris and Dr John Robey assisted me with the northern companies, Dr Jennifer Tann gave me information on source material at Birmingham, Mr Robin Chaplin and Mr T. G. Hancox made contributions on Shropshire, and Dr Arthur Raistrick on Yorkshire.

I have been very fortunate in receiving expert assistance in the preparation of illustrations. Mr Kenneth Gough and Mr James Robertson have helped with photography, particularly with copying old photographs and illustrations. Mr John Doggett has prepared maps and advised me on their presentation, and Mr Bo Lindner has made the technical drawings.

For general guidance on technical matters and presentation I am very grateful to Dr George Parker and Keith Gale, both of whom have spent valuable time in reading large sections of the manuscript and advising me on its contents. The errors which may still remain in spite of their valuable assistance are all my own, and I take full responsibility for them.

I am indebted to many others who are not mentioned here individually; but finally, I must thank my husband Roy, who has encouraged me when my energy was flagging, and assisted with almost every aspect of this work.

# Index

*Plate illustrations in italics. Main entries in bold type*

233